WHAT READERS ARE SAYING ABOUT
IT'S NOT SUPPOSED TO BE THIS WAY

"There are few people brave enough to share their truth authentically and candidly. My longtime friend Lysa TerKeurst is one of those people. In *It's Not Supposed to Be This Way*, she gives us permission to acknowledge our own pain and disappointment by courageously exposing her own. Then she points us squarely to the sovereignty and faithfulness of God. This is a powerful book not only because each chapter oozes compassion and grace but because I've personally witnessed the tears, the pain, and the prayers that produced it. And therein lies its strength. It will be impossible to read this and not be tremendously encouraged."

—Priscilla Shirer, Bible teacher and author

"My dear friend Lysa TerKeurst knows firsthand what it's like to have her faith tested to the breaking point and somehow draw closer to the Lord. I'm so grateful for her willingness to share her journey with us in *It's Not Supposed to Be This Way*. With a Job-like faith, Lysa vulnerably reveals the raw pain of enduring the unimaginable and seeking God in the midst of her struggles. This book is an instant classic on the relationship between suffering and knowing God. Not to be missed!"

—Chris Hodges, Senior Pastor, Church of the Highlands; author of *Fresh Air* and *The Daniel Dilemma*

"In *It's Not Supposed to Be This Way*, Lysa confronts the often brutal differences between the life we have and the life we expected to have with stunning vulnerability. She helps us recognize that the deep well of hurt, frustration, and discouragement cannot compare to the depth of the well of hope, joy, and restoration that God has for us. If you feel debilitated by the shackles of disappointment, then let this book point you to God's plan for a whole new way to be human. You won't get your old life back—it's much better than that."

—Levi Lusko, Pastor, Fresh Life Church; bestselling author of *Swipe Right* and *Through the Eyes of a Lion*

"Lysa encourages us that our disappointments, failures, and the unexpected can actually serve in helping us grow closer to Jesus. I would recommend anyone and everyone to pick up a copy of *It's Not Supposed to Be This Way!*"

—Chad Veach, Lead Pastor, ZOE Church LA

"This book is for every believer who has ever asked the question, 'Why, Lord?'"

—Elizabeth E.

"Lysa shares her journey through the hardest season of her life with pure honesty and a holy perspective that's relatable, tear-provoking, and life-changing."

—Ashley S.

"If you have suffered disappointment, or are currently walking through disappointment, this book is for you. It's relatable and rich with helpful Scripture. It's as if the story was my own."

—Tammy M.

"I have not read a more raw and honest book that ultimately points to God's sovereignty in the midst of life's hard. Lysa not only teaches us how to be better equipped for the fires and battles of this life, but her life illustrates how to wrestle well in the most difficult seasons. Her beautiful example of standing firm on the goodness of God—even when our flesh desperately wants to doubt and question—has been a life-changing gift to me!"

—Katie G.

"Lysa takes her own life circumstances and the Word of God and combines them into an easy-to-read and very practically applicable book! I would highly recommend this to anyone who is disappointed and struggling!"

—Erin S.

"Sometimes disappointments and hurts are so deep that a person is left feeling hopeless in the fallout of their circumstances. This book takes you on a journey of healing from that hopelessness."

—Rachel R.

IT'S NOT SUPPOSED TO BE THIS WAY

IT'S NOT SUPPOSED TO BE THIS WAY

Finding Unexpected Strength When Disappointments Leave You Shattered

LYSA TERKEURST

NELSON BOOKS

An Imprint of Thomas Nelson

Published in Nashville, Tennessee, by Nelson Books, an imprint of Thomas Nelson. Nelson Books and Thomas Nelson are registered trademarks of HarperCollins Christian Publishing, Inc.

Thomas Nelson titles may be purchased in bulk for educational, business, fund-raising, or sales promotional use. For information, please e-mail SpecialMarkets@ThomasNelson.com.

Unless otherwise noted, Scripture quotations are taken from the Holy Bible, New International Version®, NIV®. Copyright © 1973, 1978, 1984, 2011 by Biblica, Inc.® Used by permission of Zondervan. All rights reserved worldwide. www.Zondervan.com. The "NIV" and "New International Version" are trademarks registered in the United States Patent and Trademark Office by Biblica, Inc.®

Scripture quotations marked AMP are from the Amplified® Bible. Copyright © 1954, 1958, 1962, 1964, 1965, 1987 by The Lockman Foundation. Used by permission. (www.Lockman.org)

Scripture quotations marked ESV are from the ESV® Bible (The Holy Bible, English Standard Version®). Copyright © 2001 by Crossway, a publishing ministry of Good News Publishers. Used by permission. All rights reserved.

Scripture quotations marked THE MESSAGE are from The Message. Copyright © by Eugene H. Peterson 1993, 1994, 1995, 1996, 2000, 2001, 2002. Used by permission of NavPress. All rights reserved. Represented by Tyndale House Publishers, Inc.

Scripture quotations marked NASB are from New American Standard Bible®. Copyright © 1960, 1962, 1963, 1968, 1971, 1972, 1973, 1975, 1977, 1995 by The Lockman Foundation. Used by permission. (www.Lockman.org)

Scripture quotations marked NCV are from the New Century Version®. © 2005 by Thomas Nelson. Used by permission. All rights reserved.

Scripture quotations marked NKJV are from the New King James Version®. © 1982 by Thomas Nelson. Used by permission. All rights reserved.

Isaiah Institute Translation, http://www.isaiahexplained.com/16#one_col.

Any Internet addresses, phone numbers, or company or product information printed in this book are offered as a resource and are not intended in any way to be or to imply an endorsement by Thomas Nelson, nor does Thomas Nelson vouch for the existence, content, or services of these sites, phone numbers, companies, or products beyond the life of this book.

ISBN 978-0-7180-3986-8 (eBook)
ISBN 978-1-4002-1228-6 (signed)
ISBN 978-1-4002-1266-8 (signed)
ISBN 978-1-4002-1272-9 (signed)
ISBN 978-1-4002-1097-8 (IE)

Library of Congress Cataloging-in-Publication Data

Names: TerKeurst, Lysa, author.
Title: It's not supposed to be this way : finding unexpected strength when disappointments leave you shattered
/ Lysa TerKeurst.
Description: Nashville : Thomas Nelson, [2018] | Includes
bibliographical references.
Identifiers: LCCN 2018021939| ISBN 9780718039851 |
ISBN 9781400212286 (signed) | ISBN 9781400210978 (IE)
Subjects: LCSH: Disappointment--Religious aspects--Christianity. | Expectation
(Psychology)--Religious aspects--Christianity.
Classification: LCC BV4905.3 .T365 2018 | DDC 248.8--dc23 LC record available
at https://lccn.loc.gov/2018021939

Printed in the United States of America

19 20 21 22 LSC 11

To my executive team at Proverbs 31 Ministries, Meredith Brock, Lisa Allen, Barb Spencer, Glynnis Whitwer, and Danya Jordan . . . you have walked beside me every step of this journey. Words will never be able to express how grateful I am for your unconditional love, tremendous support, and fervent prayers. I love you.

And to you who hold this book right now—the hurting heart, the disappointed soul, the devastated dreamer—I know your pain. I really do. But I also know that God sees. God hears. And God loves you deeply. My prayer is that the heaviness will be lifted off of your soul as you embrace the truths through the pages of this book.

CONTENTS

INTRODUCTION

There is a favorite story I like to tell myself. It's the one about how my life should turn out. Though it's riddled with missing everyday details, it's full of a general sense of okayness. No, actually more than okayness. It's the story where my toes can dig deeply into the sands of a glorious land called *normal*. A land I didn't design but one where I'm allowed to nod in agreement before any changes occur. And I can veto all circumstances that don't look right, feel right, or smell right. My lungs inhale fresh gusts of predictability and the wind is always a gentle breeze. Never unstable or stormy and certainly not brutal or destructive.

This place is neither glamorous nor glitzy. It's casual and comfortable with a boho chic eclectic style and a pace all my own. Things don't wear out and I don't get worn down. People are kind. They do what they say they are going to do and are only grumpy enough to keep things interesting. Goodness dots the landscape like trees in bloom. Peace hovers like the best poofy clouds. And the soundtrack is simple and sweet, crescendoing with lingering laughter over all the inside jokes that a big family with so many big personalities effortlessly produces.

I like this place.

I don't want to just vacation here. I want to live here.

And I suspect you have a version of this kind of story you like to tell yourself as well.

We don't just want to read the end of our story and feel good about it. We want to take the pen and write it ourselves. We feel very certain how things should turn out. But we live in the uncertainty of neither being able to predict nor control the outcome. Humans are very attached to outcomes. We say we trust God but behind the scenes we work our fingers to the bone and our emotions into a tangled fray trying to control our outcomes. We praise God when our normal looks like what we thought it would. We question God when it doesn't. And walk away from Him when we have a sinking suspicion that God is the one who set fire to the hope that was holding us together.

Even the most grounded people can feel hijacked by the winds of unpredictable change. We feel weighed down by grief while at the same time unable to get our bearings as the weightless ashes of all we thought would be fly away.

I've never seen ashes able to control where the winds of change take them.

At least these tissue-thin pieces of debris don't expect to be able to control where they go and how they land.

I've yet to meet a human who can remain so unattached to outcomes.

We motivate ourselves to get through the bad of today by playing a mental movie of the good that will surely come tomorrow. And if not tomorrow, soon. Very soon.

And this good that comes will be such a glorious outcome that we will exhale all the anxiety and finally say, "Whew, I can honestly say it was worth it." Cue the redemption song and a small ticker tape parade.

The good outcome will look like we dreamed. It will come as

fast as we hoped it would. And it will make all the wrongs right, right, right. Those who walked faithfully with us during this hard season will feel their investment of time with us and casseroles made for us was a good one. They fulfilled yet another kingdom assignment. Check the list. And now let's all be happy.

Those who shunned you or judged you or, worst of all, somehow used your season of pain against you will see how wrong they were. They will apologize. And they will promise they learned their lesson to never ever treat anyone like that again.

This is the acceptable outcome.

This is how the formula should calculate: hard time plus healing time plus staying faithful to God should equal the exact good outcome we were counting on.

But if you are a human who has been doing the adult thing for more than twenty-four hours, you've probably come to the same stunning revelation as I have. We cannot control our outcomes. We cannot formulate how the promises of God will actually take shape. And we will never be able to demand any of the healing from all the hurt to hurry up.

I ride this struggle bus. But I'm never comfortable with the fact that I can't grab the wheel and drive it back to Normal.

I make such big assumptions of what a good God should do and then find myself epically disappointed when the winds change, the struggle bus takes a sharp turn left, and nothing at all feels right.

This isn't how I pictured my life right now.

And this probably isn't exactly how you thought things would look in your life right now either.

I'm not telling you anything new. I'm just giving voice to thoughts you've already had but maybe didn't know how to verbalize.

But, here's the hope.

Though we can't predict or control or demand the outcome of our circumstances, we can know with great certainty we will be okay. Better than okay. Better than normal. We will be victorious because Jesus is victorious (1 Corinthians 15:57). And victorious people were never meant to settle for normal.

Through these pages I'm going to help you find a soft place to land in the story God Himself is perfectly orchestrating with our good in mind. Some will live their whole lives missing the chance to see all the good God has placed around them just for them. Partly because the hard stuff has demanded so much of their attention. And the seeming permanence of some of the heartbreak has stolen their affection for life.

But what if the victory is only in part how things turn out? What if a bigger part of being victorious is how well we live today? This hour. This minute.

You are about to have a completely different experience with this thing called life. Together we will find a way to tie our hope not to the specific outcomes we thought were the only way back to normal, but rather to the very heart of God. The Author of the story your heart could never conceive but begs to live with every thumping beat. There is more to all of this than you know.

And I can't wait to watch it unfold in your life and mine.

GOING *to the* WELL

To help us on this journey as we empty ourselves of the misconceptions we have of the way life should be, I've written a section called "Going to the Well" at the end of each chapter. It's a recap of all we are learning, so we don't forget the good stuff along the way. When we empty ourselves of our misplaced hopes and limited perspectives, we have to fill ourselves up with something. So we will learn to identify our empty spaces, our thirst, and fill that void with the living water of God's truth. His Word is tailor-made to transform the hurting human heart.

Each "Going to the Well" will include statements to cling to, scriptures to soak in, questions to think on, and a prayer.

GOING *to the* WELL

Though we can't predict or control or demand the outcome of our circumstances, we can know with great certainty we will be okay.

REMEMBER (STATEMENTS TO CLING TO):

- We live in the uncertainty of neither being able to predict nor control the outcome.
- Even the most grounded people can feel hijacked by the winds of unpredictable change.
- We will be victorious because Jesus is victorious. And victorious people were never meant to settle for normal.
- What if the victory is only in part how things turn out? What if a bigger part of being victorious is how well we live today?

RECEIVE (SCRIPTURES TO SOAK IN):

But thanks be to God! He gives us the victory through our Lord Jesus Christ. (1 Corinthians 15:57)

REFLECT (QUESTIONS TO THINK ON):

- What plans or thoughts have you had about how your life should turn out?
- How do you handle not being able to control the outcome?
- In what ways do you feel you're attached to the outcome more than trusting God in the process?

Father,

I admit that so often I have held tightly to my own plans and to the outcomes that I think should come to pass. But I know the story You're writing for me is so much better than any story I could ever write for myself. Help me to cling to this truth when my circumstances are uncertain and unpredictable. I declare my trust in You above it all.

In Jesus' name, amen.

BETWE
GARDE

Chapter 1

BETWEEN TWO GARDENS

My hands were shaking as I dialed a number I'd called hundreds, if not thousands, of times before. It was 5:34 a.m. I knew the minute my friend picked up the call, the horror of what I'd just discovered would be real. I didn't want it to be real. And maybe if I kept it to myself, I could deny the hurt that was threatening to swallow me whole.

But pretending away reality never makes things better. It just causes you to implode on the inside while smiling on the outside. That's no way to live.

Sometimes to get your life back, you have to face the death of what you thought your life would look like.

I was staring that kind of death in the face when I heard my friend whisper a sleepy but slightly panicked, "Hello? Lysa? Are you okay?"

I most definitely was not.

And I wouldn't feel okay for a very long time. The feelings of safety and security in my marriage that I'd treasured for more than two decades were suddenly ripped away, leaving my heart raw and my soul trembling.

Even now, more than two years after the fact, I still struggle with the distance between what I thought would be and what is. I have days so far from okay I want to send a text message to that missing good feeling and demand its return.

Sometimes to get your life back, you have to face the death of what you thought your life would look like.

But this isn't something isolated to the white brick house that sits at the end of my driveway. This thought gets tangled around you too. It comes in like a whisper through the smaller disappointments. A bad haircut. An overflowing dishwasher. A burned dinner. A child who won't listen today. A scale that keeps going up and a bank account that keeps going down.

Then the whisper graduates into a louder voice with the friend who goes silent for a while. The job you didn't get. The harsh words spoken to you by someone you're desperate to hear some encouragement from. That underlying sense that your marriage has grown cold while your conversations are constantly heated. The lonely feeling you didn't think you'd have at this stage of life.

Then the disappointment roars with earth-shattering thunder with a call from the doctor and a diagnosis that flips life upside down. The discovered affair. The hidden addictions. The child you don't even know anymore. The fire. The bankruptcy. The breakup. The death so unexpected you keep calling their number just hoping this is all a bad dream and surely they'll answer this time.

I don't know when these disappointments, big and small, are coming my way. They just show up. An unexpected guest that I don't know what to do with.

This guest of disappointment exhausts me.

But I don't have to tell you that.

It frustrates and exhausts you too.

Life isn't turning out the way we thought it would.

Disappointment. Whether you've used that word or not, it's there. And I want to wrap a little vocabulary around the feelings that are affecting us more than we realize or dare to verbalize.

It's that feeling things should be better than they are. People should be better than they are. Circumstances should be better than they are. Finances should be better than they are. Relationships should be better than they are.

And you know what? You're right. Everything should be better than it is. It's no wonder that I'm exhausted and that you are too.

Stay with me here, and let me unpack something that Satan has viciously fought to keep us from knowing.

The disappointment that is exhausting and frustrating you? It holds the potential for so much good. But we'll only see it as good if we trust the heart of the Giver.

You see, disappointment can be a gift from God that feels nothing like a gift at all. It's unexpectedly sharp, and the Giver can seem almost cruel as we watch someone unwrap it. Their fingers will bleed. They will feel tricked and so very tempted to stop trusting that anything good can be found within. They will most certainly question the One who allowed it to come their way.

I've done all those things. I certainly threw out many deep, sob-filled questions about how God could allow this when I called my friend at 5:34 a.m.

But disappointment isn't proof that God is withholding good things from us. Sometimes it's His way of leading us Home. But to see this and properly understand what's really going on, we must take a step back and view it in the context of God's epic love story. The one in which He rescues and reconciles humanity to Himself.

So, let's lay down our questions about why these things are happening for just a bit. We'll pick them back up after we are better equipped with truths through which we can process them. And let's open up God's answers, God's ways, God's Word. I promise you won't find flimsy bumper sticker quotes that never help and often hurt. Together we are going to find a real help and a true hope and a God who will hold us safe through it all. Let's start at the very beginning.

Genesis tells us that the human heart was created in the perfection of the garden of Eden.

Can you imagine what the world looked like when God first

Disappointment

isn't proof that God is withholding good things from us. Sometimes it's His way of leading us Home.

created it? When He said it was all good. Very good. And it was all perfect.

Perfection's symphony filled the atmosphere. Everything ebbed and flowed in complete harmony. It sang with the richest tones. And danced with ridiculous precision. There was nothing that didn't look right or feel right. It was beautiful and peaceful and fulfilling. There was perfect peace in relationships. Adam and Eve were so beautifully connected to each other, and they lived in the perfect presence of God. It was paradise with unique intimacy where God would interact in direct relationship with Adam and Eve. There was perfect provision and perfect fulfillment of their purpose. There was no sadness or confusion or injustice. There was no disease or divorce or depression or death. There were no misaligned motives, no manipulations, no malicious intentions.

It was everything you could ever dream up and then so much more than that.

So the human heart was created in the context of the perfection of the garden of Eden. But we don't live there now.

This is why our instincts keep firing off the lie that perfection is possible. We have pictures of perfection etched into the very DNA of our souls.

We chase it. We angle our cameras trying to catch it. We take twenty shots in hopes of finding it. And then even our good photos have to be color corrected, filtered, and cropped.

We do our very best to make others think this posted picture is the real deal. But we all know the truth. We all see the charade. We all know the emperor is naked. But there we are, clapping on the sidelines, following along, playing the game. Trying to believe that maybe, just maybe, if we get close to something that looks like perfection it will help us snag a little of its shine for ourselves.

But we know even the shiniest of things is headed in the direction of becoming dull. New will always eventually become old. Followers unfollow. People who lift us up will let us down. The most tightly knit aspects of life snag, unravel, and disintegrate before our very eyes.

And so we are epically disappointed.

But we aren't talking about it.

We don't even feel permission to do so or we just don't know how to process our disappointments. Especially not in Bible study or Sunday church. Because everyone says, "Be grateful and positive, and let your faith boss your feelings around."

And I do believe we need to be grateful and positive and let our faith boss our feelings around. But I also think there's a dangerous aspect to staying quiet and pretending we don't get exhausted by our disappointments.

In the quiet, unexpressed, unwrestled-through disappointments, Satan is handcrafting his most damning weapons against us and those we love. It's his subtle seduction to get us alone with our thoughts so he can slip in whispers that will develop our disappointments into destructive choices.

If the enemy can isolate us, he can influence us.

And his favorite entry point of all is through our disappointments. The enemy comes in as a whisper, lingers like a gentle breeze, and builds like a storm you don't even see coming. But eventually his insatiable appetite to destroy will unleash the tornado of destruction he planned all along. He doesn't whisper to our disappointed places to coddle us. He wants to crush us.

And counselors everywhere are telling brokenhearted people sitting on tear-soaked couches that one of the reasons their relationships failed is because of conversations they needed to have but never did.

If we don't open up a way to process our disappointments, we'll be tempted to let Satan rewrite God's love story as a negative narrative, leaving us more than slightly suspicious of our Creator. Why would He create our hearts in the perfection of the garden of Eden knowing that, because of our eventual sin, we wouldn't live there?

I mean, once Adam and Eve sinned, couldn't God strip the awareness and craving for perfection out of their hearts before He banished them from the garden? Yes, He certainly could have done that. But to strip out the cause of our disappointment would also rob us of the glorious hope of where we are headed.

Remember, this is a love story. And we will never appreciate or even desire the hope of our True Love if lesser loves don't disappoint. The piercing angst of disappointment in everything on this side of eternity creates a discontent with this world and pushes us to long for God Himself—and for the place where we will finally walk in the garden with Him again. Where we will finally have peace and security and eyes that no longer leak tears . . . and hearts that are no longer broken.

The Bible begins with the book of Genesis, set in the first garden of Eden. But never forget, it ends with Eden restored in the last chapters of Revelation, the last book.

> "Look! God's dwelling place is now among the people, and he will dwell with them. They will be his people, and God himself will be with them and be their God. 'He will wipe every tear from their eyes. There will be no more death' or mourning or crying or pain, for the old order of things has passed away." He who was seated on the throne said, "I am making everything new!" (Revelation 21:3–5)

Notice all the feeling words used to describe the world we currently inhabit: *mourning, crying,* and *pain*. Utter disappointment often taps the place of deep tears. As we talked about earlier, everything on this side of eternity is in a state of decay. This is simply the natural result of sin entering the equation. Bright days become dark nights. The laughter of living will be eclipsed by the tears of dying. The excitement of this moment is torn away by the disappointment of the next moment. This constant threat to our deep feelings ushers in depression, anxiety, callousness, and, quite honestly, a skepticism about the goodness of God.

Unless.

We see that all those harsh realities aren't the end, but rather a temporary middle space. Not the place where we are meant to wallow and dwell. Rather the place through which we will have to learn to wrestle well. I need this wrestling. I have honest feelings where I want to throw my hands up in utter frustration and yell about the unfairness of it all. To deny my feelings any voice is to rob me of being human. But to let my feelings be the only voice will rob my soul of healing perspectives with which God wants to comfort me and carry me forward. My feelings and my faith will almost certainly come into conflict with each other. My feelings see rotten situations as absolutely unnecessary hurt that stinks. My soul sees it as fertilizer for a better future. Both these perspectives are real. And they yank me in different directions with never-ending wrestling. To wrestle well means acknowledging my feelings but moving forward, letting my faith lead the way.

God knows before we eternally dwell we will have to learn how to wrestle well. Do you see the encouragement God is giving us in the passage from Revelation 21 to help us do this when our feelings beg us to doubt our faith? He will stop the continuum of decay and death and utter disappointment. He will make everything new!

In this restored garden of Eden the curse will be lifted and perfection will greet us like a long-lost friend. There will be no gap between our expectations and experiences. They will be one and the same. We won't be hurt. We won't live hurt. We won't be disappointed, and we won't live disappointed. Not in people. Not in ourselves. Not in God. Our feelings and faith will nod in agreement. We will return to a purity of emotion where we can experience the best of our hearts working in tandem with the absolutes of truth.

We won't need to wrestle well between our feelings and our faith in the new Eden, because there will be no competing narrative about God's nature. There will be no corruption of God's nurture. There will be no contrary notions about why God allows things to happen. And there will be no gnawing fear that things might not turn out okay.

We won't need to wrestle well, because we will *be* well. Whole. Complete. Assured. Secure. Certain. Victorious. And brought full circle in our understanding of truth.

But, as I said at the very beginning of our discussion here, we don't live in the perfection of Eden or the yet-to-come Eden restored. Therefore, today we must understand our need to wrestle well in this space between two gardens. And we must learn to live and love in the imperfect rhythms of our clunky humanity, trying to stay on beat within a symphony of divinity.

We will get the words to the song wrong sometimes.
We will go off-key and offbeat.
We will go sharp, and we will fall flat.

But if God's symphony continues to play loud and strong as the ultimate soundtrack of our lives, we will sense how to get back on track. We will feel how to get back in rhythm. We will hear how to get back in tune.

It's just like when I sing along in my car with a well-produced song. With that soundtrack blaring along with me, I sound amazing. But it's not because I'm suddenly a master musician. It's because the master musician is louder than me, guiding me, holding me in key and on beat. I wrestle well with the song, because I'm not left on my own to hold it all together.

But heaven help us if I turn the radio down and pick up a microphone to sing it all by myself.

I won't wrestle well. I will wrangle what was beautiful music into an unrecognizable tangle of unpleasant sounds. I will add to the chaotic noise of this world, but I'll miss the glorious soundtrack meant to remind me of the epic love story I'm destined to live with the Great Lover of my soul.

So, that's the point of this book. Plain and simple. I want to learn to wrestle well in this life between two gardens. And I want to open the gift of disappointment and release the atmosphere of hope contained within. I'm so thankful we get to do this together.

GOING *to the* WELL

The human heart was created in the context of the perfection of the garden of Eden. But we don't live there now.

REMEMBER:

- Sometimes to get your life back, you have to face the death of what you thought your life would look like.
- Disappointment is that feeling things should be better than they are.
- Disappointment isn't proof that God is withholding good things from us. Sometimes it's His way of leading us Home.
- If the enemy can isolate us, he can influence us.
- We will never appreciate or even desire the hope of our True Love if lesser loves don't disappoint.
- God knows before we eternally dwell we will have to learn how to wrestle well.
- In the new Eden we won't need to wrestle well, because we will *be* well.

RECEIVE:

"Look! God's dwelling place is now among the people, and he will dwell with them. They will be his people, and God himself will be with them and be their God. 'He will wipe every tear from their eyes. There will be no more death' or mourning or crying or pain, for the old order of things has passed away." He who was seated on the throne said, "I am making everything new!" (Revelation 21:3–5)

REFLECT:

- What disappointments are you currently facing?
- Are there any long-standing untruths you've been believing about your disappointments?
- As you look back and consider the past, what gifts have come out of your disappointments?
- In what ways can you learn to wrestle well in the midst of your right-now life?
- How does this teaching on the garden of Eden help you have a better understanding of what you're going through?

Father,

Living in the messy middle between two gardens is so trying at times. Teach me to wrestle well between my faith and my feelings when life disappoints in ways I never imagined. My disappointments don't feel like a gift at all, but I'm going to trust You—the Giver of good gifts. Release an atmosphere of hope in my right-now life, I pray.

In Jesus' name, amen.

D   U

S T

Chapter 2
DUST

I grabbed my chest while tears slipped down my cheeks in an unending stream. The pain in my heart wasn't physical. But the stabbing emotional hurt was so intense I could hardly breathe. My hands were shaking. My eyes were wide with fear. My mouth felt paralyzed.

My life had gone from feeling full and whole to being obliterated beyond recognition.

I'd been hurt plenty of times in my life. But nothing like this.

After twenty-five years of marriage partnership, I had no choice but to tell my husband, "I love you. And I can forgive you. But I cannot share you."

Never had I felt more shattered and alone. And then, adding more salt to the wound, people started talking. I'd kept this hell I was walking through private, telling only a few friends and counselors. They were tender and helped me in ways I'll never be able to repay. There are some really good people on this earth. But others weren't so understanding or compassionate. And now realities and rumors were crushing me. I was experiencing the death of my "normal life." But people don't have funerals for "normal." I was dealing with extreme grief from losing the person I loved the very most in this world. But instead of visiting a gravesite and mourning a death, I was visiting the rumor mill and being devastated by all the theories and opinions. My pillow was soaked with tears of which only I knew the real source. Not only was I dealing with deep personal pain, but I was experiencing firsthand the way broken people sometimes contribute to the brokenness of others.

We live in a broken world where broken things happen. So it's not surprising that things get broken in our lives as well. But what about those times when things aren't just broken but shattered beyond repair? Shattered to the point of dust. At least when things are broken there's some hope you can glue the pieces back together.

But what if there aren't even pieces to pick up in front of you? You can't glue dust.

It's hard to hold dust. What was once something so very precious is now reduced to nothing but weightless powder even the slightest wind could carry away. We feel desperately hopeless. Dust begs us to believe the promises of God no longer apply to us. That the reach of God falls just short of where we are. And that the hope of God has been snuffed out by the consuming darkness all around us.

We want God to fix it all. Edit this story so it has a different ending. Repair this heartbreaking reality.

But what if fixing, editing, and repairing isn't at all what God has in mind for us in this shattering?

What if, this time, God desires to make something completely brand-new? Right now. On this side of eternity. No matter how shattered our circumstances may seem.

Dust is the exact ingredient God loves to use.

We think the shattering in our lives could not possibly be for any good. But what if shattering is the only way to get dust back to its basic form so that something new can be made? We can see dust as a result of an unfair breaking. Or we can see dust as a crucial ingredient.

Think about a plain piece of ice. If the ice stays in a cube, it will always be just a square of ice. But if the ice melts it can be poured into a beautiful form to reshape it when frozen again. Dust is much the same; it's the basic ingredient with such great potential for new life.

Of all the things God could have used to make man, He chose to use dust. "Then the Lord God formed a man from the dust of the ground and breathed into his nostrils the breath of life, and the man became a living being" (Genesis 2:7).

Jesus used the dust of the ground to restore a man's sight. Jesus said, "'While I am in the world, I am the light of the world.' After saying this, he spit on the ground, made some mud with the saliva, and put it on the man's eyes" (John 9:5–6). And after the man washed in the pool of Siloam, he went home seeing.

And, when mixed with water, dust becomes clay. Clay, when placed in the potter's hands, can be formed into anything the potter dreams up!

> Yet You, LORD, are our Father.
>> We are the clay, you are the potter;
>> we are all the work of your hand.
>
> (ISAIAH 64:8)

"Can I not do with you, Israel, as this potter does?" declares the LORD. "Like clay in the hand of the potter, so are you in my hand, Israel." (Jeremiah 18:6)

Dust doesn't have to signify the end. Dust is often what must be present for the new to begin.

Think about how much of an end it feels like when someone dies. No matter how well we take care of ourselves and those we love, no matter how good we are, no matter how mature in the faith we become, we will not escape the reality that death is certain and our lives will be reduced to dust. Genesis 3:19 tells us that from dust we came and to dust we shall return. That can certainly make us step back and wonder, *What is the point of all this?* In the end, we all die, decay, and decompose into dust. But for those who believe in Jesus Christ as the Lord of their lives, this isn't the end but the beginning of a transformation we all long to experience. Physical death is the only way to start the process of receiving our

Dust doesn't have to signify the end. Dust is often what must be present for the new to begin.

heavenly bodies that will never wear out, decay in any way, or ever be reduced to dust.

> For we know that when this earthly tent we live in is taken down (that is, when we die and leave this earthly body), we will have a house in heaven, an eternal body made for us by God himself and not by human hands. We grow weary in our present bodies, and we long to put on our heavenly bodies like new clothing. For we will put on heavenly bodies; we will not be spirits without bodies. While we live in these earthly bodies, we groan and sigh, but it's not that we want to die and get rid of these bodies that clothe us. Rather, we want to put on our new bodies so that these dying bodies will be swallowed up by life. God himself has prepared us for this, and as a guarantee he has given us his Holy Spirit. (2 Corinthians 5:1–5 NLT)

Remember God's declaration in Revelation 21:5 about Eden restored? *"I am making everything new!"* Death is but a passageway at God's designated time for us to finally escape this broken world full of imperfections and be welcomed to the Home we've been longing for our entire lives. We don't determine when this is, but we don't have to fear death as an end. It's another beginning.

Yes, in the restored Eden there will be no more death. No more crying. No more broken hearts or broken circumstances. No more shattered realities. No more dust. What a redeeming thought: that the shattering of our physical bodies leads us to God's renewal, where we will experience no more shattering, physical or otherwise.

When I wrote my last book, *Uninvited*, I felt I had wisdom to share on the very painful subject of rejection. God had helped me make so much progress with the painful rejections of my past that I felt certain I could help others. I pictured my reader sitting knee-deep in rejection's grief, feeling less alone because she could sense me there with her. She could rely on the fact that my teachings weren't good-sounding theories but hard-fought-for truths. She would know I'd felt the depth of her pain, so she could trust there was hope for her healing as well.

I wrote the book.
I turned it over to the editors.
I checked that assignment off my list.
Life moved on.

And then I found out about my husband's affair. Life as I knew it stopped. It turned upside down. All the best parts were shaken loose. The more I tried to grab hold of what was falling down around me, the more I realized my utter lack of control.

As I described at the beginning of this chapter, I'd been hurt plenty of times in my life, but nothing like this.

Things crashed. Things broke beyond repair. Things went from being whole to being reduced to dust. I crawled into bed. I willed the world to stop spinning. I wanted everything to pause and stop hurting me. But nothing did.

And that's one of the most devastating realities of dust times in our lives. We need the world to stop spinning for a while. We need things to pause. We need the celebrations to cease long enough to let us work through our grief. We need people with expectations to stop e-mailing us. We need our schedules to clear.

But my calendar didn't get that memo. It didn't magically erase all the things I'd agreed to do when life felt predictable and whole.

Including this book I'd written on rejection. It was due to be released in six months. But there was one final step required: I had to read through the entire manuscript one last time.

I remember getting the final page proofs of the book in the mail. They came to my house, delivered by a truck that rumbled and rushed down my long gravel driveway. The UPS man dropped the package at my front door. He rang the doorbell. He hopped back in his truck. And then he was off to his next delivery.

To that delivery man it was just another day.

Little did he know he was delivering life back into a soul hanging on by a thread.

I opened the envelope, and there it was—my book to help the world deal with the very feelings now pulsing in my heart. *Why, God, would You let me write this book when You knew I was clueless about the devastation marching in my direction? I'm the biggest fool for picking this topic. After all, I should have known I'd be attacked in the very area I was writing about. And You could have stopped me, God. You could have stopped this whole thing.*

I felt so very empty as I spread the pages across the rumpled covers of my bed.

I had nothing to give anyone. And yet, I was about to stand before the tempest-tossed world like the Statue of Liberty promising my own version of a fresh start: "Give me your broken hearts, promises not kept by others, and your fears tangled with tears yearning to breathe free. I will be a light by which you can find God's hope past the heartbreak of rejection."

When I'd first written *Uninvited*, I had been excited about talking to others about healing from the rejections of my past. But how in the world could I possibly talk about rejection when I was feeling so devastated by such a fresh wound?

I stared at the typed-out words strung together page after page.

I wanted it all to go away.

The book.

The rejection.

The timing of it all.

Yes, especially the timing. It seemed like such a cruel twist of irony.

And what was so very crazy is that in the months leading up to this devastation, the one thing I kept hearing God say to me was, "Trust my timing."

But it was the timing that seemed so very confusing. It was the timing that fed this intense awareness that no matter how well I plan things, I can't control them. No matter how well I think I know the people in my life, I can't control them. No matter how well I follow the rules, do what's right, and seek to obey God with my whole heart, I can't control my life. I can't control God.

It's hard to type those words.

Because I don't want to control God.

Until I do.

When His timing seems questionable, His lack of intervention seems hurtful, and His promises seem doubtful, I get afraid. I get confused. And left alone with those feelings, I can't help but feel disappointed that God isn't doing what I assume a good God should do.

I want to assume that God would have seen the rejection coming my way and stopped me from writing on that topic. Or better yet, I want to assume God would have intervened and prevented this rejection from happening in the first place. I want to assume that His promise to never leave me or forsake me means that He's operating like a supernatural shield around me, preventing horrific things from happening to me and those I love.

I want to assume that my definition of best should be God's definition of best. And that my definition of good should be God's definition of good.

I want to write the story of my life according to all my assumptions.

Therefore, it's impossible to escape the truth that I don't want to relinquish control to God. I want to take control from God.

And then I make the most dangerous assumption of all: I could surely do all of this better than God.

Of course, I don't ever verbalize any of that. But there it is. I picture Satan standing there, luring me in. He has *control* written on one of his hands and *disappointment* on the other. He holds out control and says, "Take control of your own life. Stop following God's rules. When you're in control you'll be able to get everything you've ever felt denied by God." And with his other hand he starts pointing to all the many disappointments of my life and questions, "Why would God keep good things from you? He's such a restrictive God. His rules really shouldn't apply to your situation. You actually know better."

Disappointment happens every time I come face-to-face with my absolute inability to control people, circumstances, and timing. If I could control all these things, I'd arrange my own version of perfection. I'd be the boss of my life and those in my life.

And I'd do exactly what Adam and Eve did. I'd have a love affair with my own desires. I'd sell my soul for a lie laced with poison.

The very things I assume would give me a better life are the exact things that would eventually kill me.

Look at the dangerous progression that happened with Eve:

In Genesis 2:16, God's first three words to Adam when telling him the rule of not eating from the tree of the knowledge of good and evil were, "You are free." God gave him a message of freedom with one restriction for his protection.

But when the serpent quoted this rule to Eve, he changed God's language of freedom to complete restriction with no freedom at all. When quoting God, the serpent's first three words were, "You must not" (Genesis 3:1). And then he finished by exaggerating the rule to say Adam and Eve must not eat from *any* tree in the garden.

Eve heard the mistake and corrected the serpent, but then added her own restriction that was a complete misquote of God's rule: "We may eat fruit from the trees in the garden, but God did say, 'You must not eat fruit from the tree that is in the middle of the garden, and you must not touch it, or you will die'" (Genesis 3:2–3).

God never said anything about touching the fruit. And He certainly didn't say if they touched it they would die.

She assumed this.

Please see how dangerous this assumption was. She got alone with her own thoughts and assumptions. And it led her to doubt God. And take control to get what she wanted. What she thought was best.

And do you see how the serpent played into this? "You will not certainly die . . . For God knows that when you eat from it your eyes will be opened, and you will be like God, knowing good and evil" (Genesis 3:4–5).

In other words, "Eve, it's not a bad thing to want to be like God, is it? Why would God keep this from you?"

I don't want to assign her a thought that we can't see verified in Scripture, but her disobedience seems to point to the same struggle I have when I don't like God's plan: *surely I could do this better than God.*

Genesis 3:6 says, "When the woman saw that the fruit of the tree was good for food and pleasing to the eye, and also desirable for gaining wisdom, she took some . . ."

Don't miss this. Before she ate it, she took it. She touched it, and she didn't die.

Then she ate it. And gave some to Adam, who was with her and who also saw that Eve didn't die when she touched it, so he ate some. And sin entered in.

Do you see how dangerous that misquote, that misunderstanding of God's instruction, was? Eve's assumption that she would die when she touched the fruit seemed to prove God wrong. And it reinforced the lie of the serpent that she could be like God. She didn't die. So, maybe she did know better. This very dangerous perception could have helped her justify the next step of eating the fruit. This is the progression of sin. And this wasn't just a personal tragedy for Eve and Adam. It ushered in a horrific reality for all of humanity.

Perfection ended.

Curses began.

Consequences were unleashed.

And they were banished from the garden.

Spiritual death was immediate.

Physical death was imminent.

From dust they came, and now to dust they would return.

But here's the good news: even when we follow in Eve's footsteps, when we try to take control and make assumptions and misunderstand God on every level, He still has a plan. A good plan. A plan to make something from dust.

And eventually we will understand that God hasn't denied us the best. He's offering us the very best by offering Himself. He is our only source of perfection on this side of eternity. And He sees a perfect plan for our dust.

We may be afraid of all the disappointment of this broken world. But God isn't afraid. He's aware. So very aware of His ultimate plans and purposes. It isn't to keep us from getting shattered. It's to keep our souls connected, so deeply connected to Himself.

And let's be honest, if we weren't ever disappointed, we'd settle for the shallow pleasures of this world rather than addressing the spiritual desperation of our souls. We don't think about fixing things until we realize they are broken. And even then we don't call in the experts until we surrender to the realization we cannot fix things on our own. If our souls never ached with disappointments and disillusionments, we'd never fully admit and submit to our need for God. If we weren't ever shattered we'd never know the glorious touch of the Potter making something glorious out of dust, out of us.

It took me forever to focus enough to read the first couple of paragraphs of *Uninvited*. And then the first couple of pages turned into the first couple of chapters. Tears slid down my face and dripped onto my shirt. I pressed the loose pages into my chest.

God had given me the book last year I'd be so desperate to read this year.

That reader I'd imagined? She was me.

Maybe the timing and the subject matter of my book wasn't a cruel twist of irony.

Maybe it was just right. For me and my situation. And for everyone else who would soon encounter *Uninvited*.

And maybe the freshness of my own rejection would make the message I'd soon be delivering that much more authentic. I wouldn't be teaching only from past experiences but from an even deeper awareness of just how painful the healing process can be.

I wouldn't have written my story this way. I would have avoided anything that looks like dust. I think we all would.

Let's revisit that paragraph I wrote earlier.

When His timing seems questionable, His lack of intervention seems hurtful, and His promises seem doubtful, I get afraid. I get confused. And left alone with those feelings, I can't help but feel disappointed that God isn't doing what I assume a good God should do.

There isn't any timing that seems like the right timing to be shattered into dust.

There isn't any plan God could present where I would willingly agree to be broken into unglueable pieces.

I just wouldn't.

And what a tragedy that would be. My controlling things would prevent the dust required for God to make the new He desperately desires for me. And isn't that what all His promises hinge on? Old becoming new. Dead things coming to life. Good from evil. Darkness turning to light.

If I want His promises, I have to trust His process.

If I want His promises, I have to trust His process.

I have to trust that first comes the dust, and then comes the making of something even better with us. God isn't ever going to forsake you, but He will go to great lengths to remake you.

What if disappointment is really the exact appointment your soul needs to radically encounter God?

GOING *to the* WELL

Dust doesn't have to signify the end. Dust is often what must be present for the new to begin.

REMEMBER:

- We live in a broken world where broken things happen.
- Dust is the exact ingredient God loves to use.
- God speaks in a language of freedom; Satan speaks in a language of restriction.
- God is our only source of perfection on this side of eternity. And He sees a perfect plan for our dust.
- If I want His promises, I have to trust His process.
- God isn't ever going to forsake you, but He will go to great lengths to remake you.
- What if disappointment is really the exact appointment your soul needs to radically encounter God?

RECEIVE:

Yet You, LORD, are our Father.
We are the clay, you are the potter;
we are all the work of your hand.
(Isaiah 64:8)

Also read:
Genesis 2—3
Jeremiah 18:6
John 9:5–6
2 Corinthians 5:1–5
Revelation 21:5

REFLECT:

- When has your life felt shattered to the point of dust?
- How do you relate to the story of Adam and Eve's disobedience?
- Where are you hoping for a new beginning?
- In what ways are you willing to trust God's process for your life?

Father,

This world is broken and broken things happen—yes. Even still, I can't help but feel utterly shattered and disillusioned when heartbreak is a part of my story. I don't like this—I don't like dust. But dust is one of Your favorite ingredients to use when making something new, and I believe You are working right now to do this very thing in my life. I know You will never forsake me, but that You will go to great lengths to remake me. Thank You.

In Jesus' name, amen.

BUT HOW

THROUGH

NEXT 86

SECONDS

DO I GET

THE

400

?

Chapter 3

BUT HOW DO I GET THROUGH
THE NEXT 86,400 SECONDS?

*O*kay, so dust is what I have in front of me. And a glorious remaking is what's ahead of me. But how do we fix the pain of today? Because I've got 86,400 seconds of today I have to get through. So, what's the plan to help me not hurt today?" I looked the counselor straight in the eye and willed myself not to blink.

I wanted a step-by-step plan to get me through this. I wanted a guarantee that if I followed the plan, then the pain would go away. And if he couldn't give me all that, then I wanted a pill. A pill to help me sleep through the next year, so I could just wake up on the other side of this with everything miraculously fixed.

I always want miraculous fixes without pain.

Just a few days ago I posted a picture on Instagram. I was covered in sweat. But not like the sweat those perfectly airbrushed athletic girls have in the ads for activewear. The ones where the girls are jumping hurdles, or running marathons, or participating in a spin class with smiles on their faces. Their sweat glistens on top of perfectly toned muscles that scream, "I don't eat pizza, I live for workouts, and I don't even own a Spanx undergarment of any kind."

Awesome. I totally relate to that girl. In absolutely no way at all.

My sweat is more like, "Bless her heart. She tries." My makeup was smeared all over the place. It's so attractive to see your colored-in eyebrows dripping down your cheeks.

So, I posted the picture with this caption: "The workout situation. Have mercy. Can someone invent a machine where I just lie down while it moves my body, burns all the calories, and whispers in my ear how amazing I'm about to look?!" More than three hundred people chimed in to please let them know if I found this machine. Because, hello, we all want quick results with no pain.

My counselor didn't give me a quick fix. I'm sure he wanted

to. I'm sure he wished he had some fix-it formula he could sprinkle over me and my five hundred snot tissues. For real. I cried so hard in some of our sessions that I found myself twisting the corners of the tissues into cones I could insert in my nostrils to just stop the flow. It wasn't so noticeable while my hand was pressed with the tissue against my nose. But my animated expressions would inevitably demand I use my hands to demonstrate something with great emotion. This left the cone-shaped tissues inserted into my nostrils just hanging there from my face.

You know that awkward feeling you get when talking with someone who has something in her teeth? You can hardly concentrate on what she is saying, because "Girl, you don't even know how ridiculous you look right now, and I want to tell you but I just keep hoping that your tongue will catch hold of whatever that is and you'll just swallow the thing."

I'm sure my counselor missed half of whatever I was saying, because "Girl, don't you realize how hard it is to stay in the empathetic counselor zone when you have a twisted tissue hanging from your nostril?!"

So, yes, I'm sure he wanted to fix a lot about me. Especially my desire for everything to be okay right now and my refusal to just embrace the process of healing.

I knew God would eventually make everything okay.

I knew God would, in fact, make something new and wonderful from my dust. I just didn't know how to function without freaking out in the midst of daily life. Like when I laid my head down on the banana display in the grocery store, completely spent. I was just standing there with an empty cart, a heart full of pain, and my face pressed into the display. The teenage worker saw me and couldn't figure out what I was doing. I guess he assumed my concern was about the choices of fruit before me. So, heaven help him, he asked,

"Can I help you?" I turned my face toward him. Tears flooded out. And all I could think to say was, "I need a tissue."

Whether you're a counselor or an underpaid fruit attendant at the grocery store, it's utterly exhausting to be with someone with so much emotion and so many twisted tissues.

My counselor finally broke the news to me that there was simply no easy way around the heartbreaking circumstances in my marriage. I would have to walk through them. And it would be painful.

Feeling the pain is the first step toward healing the pain. The longer we avoid the feeling, the more we delay our healing. We can numb it, ignore it, or pretend it doesn't exist, but all those options lead to an eventual breakdown, not a breakthrough.

The longer we avoid the feeling, the more we delay our healing.

The feeling of the pain is like a warning light on the dashboard of our car. The light comes on to indicate something is wrong. We can deny it. We can ignore it. We can assume it's a little glitch in the operating panel. We can even go to the mechanic and ask him to turn off that annoying little light. But if he's a good mechanic, he would tell you it's foolish not to pay attention to it. Because if you don't attend to it, you will soon experience a breakdown. The warning light isn't trying to annoy you. It's trying to protect you.

And pain is much the same. It's the pain we feel that finally demands we slow down enough to address what's really going on below the surface.

I don't know what pain you are going through today. But I suspect whatever it is, it's got some roots of disappointment. You didn't think life would be like this. You didn't think circumstances would be like this. You didn't think you'd be like this. You didn't think they would be like this. You didn't think God would be like this.

Depending on the level of pain, you'll use different words to describe the feelings. Words I've already used throughout these pages. Words like: *disillusioned, devastated, let down,* or *driven to the brink of utter frustration.* Whatever it is, the roots of all these feelings can be traced back to disappointment. You are expressing that your experience of life isn't matching your expectations of how you thought your life would be.

Those feelings are painful. And that pain must be addressed.

God helped me see this in a pretty dramatic way last summer.

I woke up on what I thought would be an ordinary Monday last June. But nothing was normal. I felt as if knives were mercilessly carving their way through my insides. Waves of nausea left me convulsing and desperate for relief. I tried to step out of bed, but I collapsed. I screamed.

My family rushed me to the emergency room where we all hoped I could find some relief and help. It would be five excruciatingly horrible and exhausting days before I'd find either. I never knew how impossible it could feel to live another hour much less another day. I never knew how painful even sixty seconds could be. I never desperately desired death before as my only option for relief.

But lying in the critical care unit—an abdomen distending more and more with each passing hour, tubes running in and out of a body refusing to function, and a pain pump set to deliver the highest doses but still not relieving the pain—will make death look quite appealing.

I had gone from feeling just fine traveling home from vacation on Sunday to lying drenched in tears and sweat in the critical care unit on Monday.

What in the world?! I mean, my stomach had been hurting off and on in varying degrees for years. But the pain would always go away, and I would brush it off thinking it was something I ate or some little virus. But this pain couldn't be brushed off or ignored. It consumed me.

At first, my mind couldn't think rationally at all. I was just panicked, trying to figure out how to get immediate relief from my pain. I was in the urgency of the moment. But as the panic started to give way to desperation, I cried out for God to help me. "Take the pain away! Please, dear God, take this pain away!"

But He didn't. Not that moment. Not the next. Not even the next day.

His silence stunned me.

How could God do that? How could He say I'm His daughter whom He deeply loves but let me lie there in excruciating pain? I have children. And if I could take away their pain, without a doubt I would. God could do that. But He was choosing not to.

C. S. Lewis wrote, "I believe in Christianity as I believe that the Sun has risen: not only because I see it, but because by it I see everything else."[1]

I like that quote. It's certainly Facebook-worthy. But in the context of my hospital bed, when the darkness of pain seemed to block out any sliver of light, a rebellious doubt drummed inside my head: *What do you see now?*

I saw pain. I saw myself desperately crying out to God. I saw no evidence that God was doing anything with my cries. I saw painful minutes turn into hours and then turn into days. I saw doctors scratching their heads. I saw tears in my mom's eyes.

I saw fear in my family's eyes. I saw bewilderment in my friends' eyes.

But I didn't see God doing anything about any of this.

And isn't that what deeply troubles us about this whole relationship thing we're encouraged to have with God? Doesn't a relationship mean you show up when needed?

Few things affect me more than being disappointed by those people who love me.

But being disappointed by the fact that God doesn't seem to be showing up during times of my greatest need?

That wrecks my soul.

It's not that I expect God to fix everything about my situation. But I do expect Him to do something.

I kept picturing Him standing beside my bed seeing my anguish, watching my body writhing in pain, hearing my cries but making the choice to do nothing. And I couldn't reconcile that.

It's the same thing that happens when I hear of a baby being stillborn. Or a young mother dying of cancer. Or a teenager committing suicide. Or someone suffering in a refugee camp. Or people starving in a third-world country.

Where are You, God?

I mean, even humans with the slightest bit of compassion are compelled to do something to help another person in deep distress and pain.

A few years ago my husband and I witnessed a terrible car accident. Without even thinking, our instincts were immediately to help. I started praying while Art jumped out of our truck, raced over to one of the cars, and pulled the unconscious driver away from the smoking wreckage. Blood was everywhere. There were shards of glass and mangled metal. And no guarantees any of this was safe to do. But something inside had compelled us to pull over.

We didn't even know these people. We never even found out their names.

But we couldn't just drive by and do nothing. I don't say this to shine some sort of halo over our heads. I'm just saying, as imperfect as we are, we were compelled to do something.

So, how can a perfect God seemingly stay silent at times?

We Christians rally around these unexplainable horrors with Bible verses and sermon points and well-meaning clichés, but in the less-trusting places of our brains, we tilt our gaze and scratch our heads. *God, this really doesn't add up. How do I see all this senseless suffering and still sing about You being a good, good Father? It adds so much fuel to the fire of skeptics. And quite honestly makes me cry. I don't want to question You. But it's hard when I'm so utterly disappointed. It feels like You're not showing up here.*

After five of the longest and most excruciating days of my life, a new doctor came to my hospital room dressed in scrubs and prepped for surgery. He'd run one last test. And, finally, we had some answers. The right side of my colon had ripped away from the abdominal wall and twisted around the left side. The blood flow was completely cut off. My colon had distended from the normal four centimeters in diameter to more than fourteen centimeters. It had been in danger of rupturing when it was around ten centimeters, at which point I would have felt relief from the intense pain. And it's at that exact time when many others suffering with this medical situation feel that relief and go to sleep. Their bodies turn septic, and they die.

The surgeon explained that he needed to rush me into emergency surgery and he'd be removing most of my colon. He was hoping to save enough that my body would eventually be able to function properly, but he wasn't sure. He wasn't even sure I'd make it through the surgery.

And with that daunting news, I hugged my family, prayed with my pastor, and was wheeled into the surgical unit.

Weeks later, while I was home recovering, the surgeon called me. He'd gotten the report back from the mass that was removed, and there was no further treatment needed. However, there was an alarming part of the report he couldn't reconcile, even with his years of practicing medicine.

He said, "Lysa, I don't really like how people throw around the term *miracle*. But honestly, it's the only word I know to use in your case. The cells in your colon were already in a state of autolysis. This is where your brain has signaled your body to start self-digesting. It's decomposition. It's what happens when you die. Lysa, you can't get any closer to death than that. How you survived this, I can't explain."

I hung up the phone, stunned. And I suddenly thought of those days before the surgery when I was begging God to take away the pain. I had questioned God because of the pain. I had wondered how God could let me be in so much pain. And I had cried, because I thought God somehow didn't care about my pain.

But in the end, it was the pain that God used to save my life.

The pain was what kept me in the hospital. The pain was what kept me demanding the doctors run more tests. The pain was what forced me to address what desperately needed to be attended to within my body. The pain was what made me allow a surgeon to cut my belly wide open. The pain was what helped save me.

Had God taken away the pain, I would have gone home, my colon would have ruptured, my body would have turned septic, and I would have died.

I now have a completely different picture of God standing beside my hospital bed while I was hurting and begging Him to help me. He wasn't ignoring me. No, I believe it took every bit of holy restraint within Him to not step in and remove my pain. He loved me too much to do the very thing I was begging Him to do. He knew things I didn't know. He saw a bigger picture I couldn't see. His mercy was too great. His love was too deep.

Indeed, He is a good, good Father.

My colon had been in trouble for a while. My stomach had been hurting for a while. But the pain hadn't been severe enough to force me to address what was happening below the surface.

This isn't just true of physical pain. It's true of emotional pain as well. The emotional pain from the last chapter was also something brewing for a couple of years. But I couldn't put my finger on it. I didn't know exactly what I was dealing with. I discerned that something wasn't right, but discernment doesn't always give details. Once the truth surfaced, the pain was so intense I couldn't ignore it any longer. I had to do something about it. I needed God's help.

And God longs to help us.

Stop right here, and personalize that statement. Say it out loud: "God longs to help me."

Now, keep this statement in the context of how God longs to help us. There are many things God longs to help us with, but at the core of it all, He longs to help us through the process of being made into the image of Christ. He is our ultimate example of wrestling well between divine faith and human feelings, so the more we become like Him, the more we learn to trust God, no matter what our human eyes can see.

During the days of Jesus' life on earth, he offered up prayers and petitions with fervent cries and tears to the one who could save him from death, and he was heard because of his reverent submission. Son though he was, he learned obedience from

what he suffered and, once made perfect, he became the source
of eternal salvation for all who obey him. (Hebrews 5:7–9)

Please don't rush past this heart-stopping truth. Jesus learned
obedience from what He suffered. He was fully God but also fully
human. His divinity was complete but His humanity grew and
matured and learned how to be obedient.

It would take a lot of obedience to do life with humans who
were so fickle, forgetful, disrespectful, untrusting, and unbending
with their pride. It would take a lot of obedience to love people
who spit on Him, mocked Him, and wronged Him in every way.
It would take a lot of obedience to go to the cross for these people.
For all people. For you and me.

His humanity suffered. Really suffered. Hear the raw angst in
this reality: "He offered up prayers and petitions with fervent cries
and tears to the one who could save Him from death."

His humanity said, please not this.

His humanity cried for something different.

His humanity begged for another way.

But this obedience He learned from suffering compelled Him
to trust God beyond what His physical eyes could see.

*Oh, dear God, help me trust You beyond what my physical eyes
can see. As the winds of all that's uncontrollable whip around
me and thrash against me, I need something to ground me.
Steady me. Hold me together when circumstances are falling
apart. I want to trust You beyond what my eyes can see.*

Can you imagine how much less anxiety, fear, angst, and heartbreak we would have if we could truly trust God? I don't mean just
saying we trust God because it's the Christian thing to say. I don't

mean just singing words of trusting God because it's in the praise song. I mean having a marked moment. A real live moment we can point to and remind ourselves that we declared we will trust God with this suffering. With this disappointment. With this situation.

Jesus had many marked moments. We often read how Jesus got away to pray and be with His heavenly Father. He would face something and need a marked moment with His Father to trade His human desire for God's will. We read about one of the most memorable of these marked moments in Mark 14, when He asked God, "Take this cup from me." His humanity wanted a different plan, but He marked His request with the ultimate statement of trusting God: "Yet not what I will, but what you will" (Mark 14:36).

When Jesus taught us to pray, He modeled again marked moments of trust on a daily basis.

This, then, is how you should pray:

"Our Father in heaven,
hallowed be your name,
your kingdom come,
your will be done,
on earth as it is in heaven.
Give us today our daily bread."

(MATTHEW 6:9–11)

This is obedience. This is trust. Obedience is the daily practice of trusting God. So, the only way to gain the kind of trust in God we must have to survive and thrive in this life between two gardens is through the things that we suffer.

Suffering. The very thing that makes us wonder if God is cruel.

The very thing that makes us question God's goodness. The very thing I couldn't understand in that hospital bed. The very thing I don't want to be part of God's plan ever, ever, ever. Not for me. Not for you. Not for any human.

But here's the craziest thing of all. God doesn't want you or me to suffer. But He will allow it in doses to increase our trust. Our pain and suffering isn't to hurt us. It's to save us. To save us from a life where we are self-reliant, self-satisfied, self-absorbed, and set up for the greatest pain of all . . . separation from God.

Think about why we will yank a child back from running across a street. The initial jerk back may cause the child some pain and confusion. But that tiny bit of suffering is for the greater good of saving the child from the worse suffering of getting hit by a car.

The situation with my colon caused me lots of pain and confusion. But it was for the greater good of saving me from a colon rupture and possibly death.

To trust God is to trust His timing. To trust God is to trust His way. God loves me too much to answer my prayers at any other time than the right time and in any other way than the right way. In the quietness of all that doesn't feel right, this truth does.

So I say it again and my suffering today isn't so intense. This truth calms me.

God loves me too much to answer my prayers at any other time than the right time and in any other way than the right way.

This doesn't change the fact that I want all of this to go away. I want happy. I want normal. I want easy. I want to wake up tomorrow morning with my husband's arms around me, as he assures me that it was all just a bad dream. That's what I want. Because that's all I can conceive as a good plan.

However, God sees things I can't see. He knows things I don't know. Only God knows what the good plan is and what it will take

God *loves* me too

much to answer my

prayers at any other

time than the right

time and in any other

way than the right way.

to get me there. And most of all He knows, if I saw the full road ahead, I would stop about halfway through and never choose to continue with His plan. I would think the cost is too high, the path too scary, the way too daunting, and the enemy too frightening. No human is strong enough to withstand seeing too much of God's plan in advance. It must be revealed daily. And we must be led to it and through it slowly.

Jesus is the perfect one to show us the way, the truth, and the life. The one who understands how hard the 86,400 seconds of one day can be. God doesn't just stand back while we are suffering and say, "Good luck. I hate that you're in pain, but welcome to the reality of living in a sin-soaked world. Hang on. Deal with it. Eventually, I'll do something good with it all."

No.

God sent His Son Jesus to be His help with skin on.

Jesus came to share in our humanity. To feel what we feel. To hurt like we hurt. To suffer like we suffer. To be tempted like we are tempted. To defeat what we fear. To set us free from the curse of sin and death. And to lead us through this life between two gardens.

> Since the children have flesh and blood, he too shared in their humanity so that by his death he might break the power of him who holds the power of death—that is, the devil—and free those who all their lives were held in slavery by their fear of death . . . For this reason he had to be made like them, fully human in every way, in order that he might become a merciful and faithful high priest in service to God, and that he might make atonement for the sins of the people. Because he himself suffered when he was tempted, he is able to help those who are being tempted. (Hebrews 2:14–15, 17–18)

But don't miss the very next verse! The very next sentence! This is our answer when we are standing at the bruised bananas display with a heart so battered we just can't take it any longer. Or when you are lying in a hospital bed with nothing to stare at but confused doctors and a pain pump that isn't even taking the edge off the pain of your convulsing stomach.

We don't need to stare at the bewildered fruit dude or the baffled doctors. We have a place to look. We have a Savior to look to.

> Therefore, holy brothers and sisters, who share in the heavenly calling, fix your thoughts on Jesus, whom we acknowledge as our apostle and high priest. (Hebrews 3:1)

To fix our thoughts on Jesus is to close our eyes. To mark this moment by declaring our trust in God. To declare to God out loud like Jesus did, "Not my will but Yours be done." To stop fixating on the circumstances raging around us. To stop trying to make sense of things that make no sense in the middle of the journey. And to stop asking for the knowledge that's too heavy for us to carry.

That's why God didn't want Adam and Eve to eat from the tree of the knowledge of good and evil. The knowledge it would give them was a burden God never wanted them to carry. And maybe that's why we don't have all the answers about our situations. God isn't trying to be distant or mysterious or hard to understand. He's being merciful.

We don't have to know the plan to trust there is a plan.

We don't have to feel good to trust there is good coming.

We don't have to see evidence of changes to trust that it won't always be this hard.

We just have to close our physical eyes and turn our thoughts to Jesus. Fix our thoughts on Him. Say His name over and over and over. God doesn't want to be explained away. He wants to be invited in.

And right now He's looking for someone, anyone, who will really call on Him.

In the midst of this cruel, crazy world, there you'll be . . . the one who, out of all this world, is brave enough to trust and call on the name of Jesus. You're learning disappointments aren't a reason to run away. They are the reason to turn a different way. A way few ever find.

Turn from the deep desire to know all the answers. To see too much of the plan. To carry a weight you weren't ever supposed to carry.

Make a different choice than Eve did. She demanded all the knowledge right away in her own way while ignoring God's way. If only she would have noticed that other tree. The tree of life. The tree of God's best way and perfect provision. It was there for her. She had a choice.

And so do we.

Scripture reminds us that "hope deferred makes the heart sick, but a longing fulfilled is a tree of life" (Proverbs 13:12).

Wow.

The tree of the knowledge of good and evil may not be in our physical sight today, but Satan is certainly making use of that same sense of disappointment, of our hope deferred. He wants us to be so consumed with our unmet expectations that our hearts just get sicker and sicker. He wants our inner selves to get more and more disillusioned with our circumstances, other people, and God. He wants our pain to get more and more intense to the point we lose sight of Jesus completely. And death seems appealing.

All the while Jesus is saying, "Don't deny My wounds, the healing I died to give you. Eve turned to the wrong tree and received death. I hung on a tree to bring you back to life. I am the fulfillment of your longing. I am your Tree of Life."

Charles Spurgeon once preached, "My dear friends, you will never see the tree of life aright unless you first look at the cross. . . . Thus then, Jesus Christ hanging on the cross is the tree of life in its wintertime."[2]

In the darkest hour this world has ever known, Jesus died on a cross, on a tree, as Galatians 3:13 puts it in the New Living Translation. But just as we know that trees in the wintertime only appear to be dead, so there was a redemptive transformation at work as Jesus hung on the cross.

Your life may be dark today. But make no mistake, there is a powerful work happening.

Jesus is in the process of turning your hurt into wisdom. And this wisdom will be life! Jesus is saying to us, "Nothing you desire compares to this wisdom. I will turn your pain to peace. I will turn your heartbreak into honor. And it will be worth it."

So I walk away from the banana display at the grocery store and apologize to the fruit dude. I don't need answers. I need Jesus. I need His wisdom to be the loudest voice in my life right now. I need His truth washing over my wounds right now. I must stop the madness of my own assessments and assumptions. My soul was made for assurance. And that, my friend, is exactly what God gives us.

Even when we don't understand. Even when things don't make sense. And especially when we are disappointed.

And please don't misunderstand—I'm not saying any of this is easy or tidy. Pain still hurts.

There are other people who have had the same medical emergency I had, only they didn't survive. Then there are all the other horrors and heartbreaks and inhumane conditions happening this very second all over the world. Unexplainable. Unfathomable. And unspeakable pain.

All I have to do is stand at the gravesite of my sister who died way too young and in way too much pain to be reminded that none of this is easy or tidy. Some things won't be fixed on this side of eternity; they just have to be walked through.

But when my brain begs me to doubt God—as it most certainly does—I find relief for my unbelief by laying down my human assessments and assumptions. I turn from the tree of knowledge and fix my gaze on the tree of life. I let my soul be cradled by God's divine assurance. His Son. Who completely understands. And who will walk me through every step of this if I keep my focus on Him.

That's how I survive the 86,400 seconds called today.

GOING *to the* WELL

God loves me too much to answer my prayers at any other time than the right time and in any other way than the right way.

REMEMBER:

- God will eventually make everything okay.
- The longer we avoid the feeling, the more we delay our healing.
- God doesn't want to be explained away; He wants to be invited in.
- Disappointments aren't a reason to run away. They are the reason to turn a different way.
- I find relief for my unbelief by laying down my human assessments and assumptions.

RECEIVE:

Hope deferred makes the heart sick,
but a longing fulfilled is a tree of life.
(Proverbs 13:12)

Also read:
Proverbs 13:12
Matthew 6:9–11
Mark 14:36
Hebrews 2:14–15, 17–18; 3:1; 5:7–9

REFLECT:

- Which of your prayers are going seemingly unanswered by God?
- How are you inviting the Lord into your everyday situations, and how can you improve in drawing near to Him?
- God is powerfully at work in your life and situation. What would it look like for you to rest in that truth today?

Father,

You are so very good. You can be trusted. Help me mark the hard moments of this day with declarations of my trust in You. There is more to what I'm facing today than what my physical eyes can see. When my pain feels too deep and when I don't think I can take one more second of suffering, help me recognize Your plan and protection. Help me trade my unbelief for the beautiful relief that I don't have to figure this out. I just have to fix my thoughts on Jesus and how He will lead me. I mark this moment as a moment of trust. I declare I don't have to understand. I just have to trust.

In Jesus' name, amen.

TAN

FEET

Chapter 4
TAN FEET

$\mathcal{S}$omeone made a comment to me the other day about my feet being tan. I didn't know what to say back. "Thank you" seemed awkward. I mean, a comment like that could go one of many ways. I wasn't sure if it was a subtle inquiry to figure out if I just hadn't washed my feet in a while, so what appeared tan was actually dirty? Or did they think I had possibly ventured way, way outside my box and got a spray tan? Or did I have feet that had not worn shoes in so long that the sun had access to them for real?

The answer is the latter.

So, I simply replied, "When your life doesn't require shoes, your feet get tan."

I didn't intend to sound pitiful. Or profound. I was just being honest. Probably more honest than either of us even knew. There was some nervous laughter between us, and some exchange about praying for me. And that was that.

I looked down at my feet and declared this to be a good moment. Not epic. Not evidence of profound healing. Just a moment of good. Yes, I had stood long enough in the sun without all the props and pretensions of dressing up an outside that is hurting on the inside.

And that's when it occurred to me that if you get desperate enough you'll go all in with living slow for a while. You'll quiet down all the outside noise so God's voice can become the loudest voice in your life. Now, I realize, none of us can just quit life when life falls apart. But we can quit some things.

I cut out almost all TV and social media.

I cut out reading things online and chose to read God's Word more than ever before.

I cut through the deafening silence of emptiness in my life by filling my home with praise music.

I cut out as many extra activities as possible and spent more time outside with my kids and friends who came to visit.

I cut out having lots of conversations with curious people and intentionally sought out pastoral counseling and friends with whom I knew I was safe to have deep conversations.

I cut out my speaking engagements and pouring myself out for others in this season so I could have time to be poured into.

And, I discovered something wonderful.

When you suffer, slow becomes necessary. Slow becomes good. One of the best parts of this season of suffering for me was a life that doesn't require shoes. When you wear no shoes the sun has access to your feet.

And on a spiritual level it seemed to have some sort of parallel meaning. When you live slow for a season, the Son has access to the parts of you normally covered up by everyday put-ons.

We put on impressive job titles to show the world that we've got something big going on. We put on humble brags to covertly prove how great we are, but in that quiet, God-did-it-all-but-so-did-I kind of way. We put on "one up" comments to compete with others, but all with sly comparison innuendoes. We put on God theories and higher-than-thou opinions about others to cover up our own desperate and depraved areas in need of attention.

We just aren't into taking our shoes off long enough for our feet to get tan.

We just aren't into being exposed.

We just aren't into facing the fears of stripping off all the cover-ups.

When life blew completely apart for me, not only did my greatest fear come true but my private devastation was publicly exposed. Crying in the quietness of my bedroom was much less terrifying than having people's thoughts about my family's devastation being freely discussed on the World Wide Web. Tear-soaked pillows don't shame you with their opinions, debate your sanity or spiritual maturity, or armchair quarterback all you should have done better.

But people do.

Not all people. But some really loud and proud people. People who deflect their own need for redemption by spotlighting the hurts of others. Make no mistake, those who are the most eager to harshly criticize others are often the ones most desperate to keep hidden their own secret sins or unresolved pain.

I'm all for people challenging me with biblical wisdom and considerations birthed in real prayer. But these are conversations that should be had face-to-face with compassionate lips, not articles typed with cold fingertips. And not sidebar conversations laced with judgment but masked with "let's pray for her."

The majority of people were kind and compassionate, respectful and prayerful, when they found out about the heartbreak my family had been experiencing. But it only takes a few loud talkers to hijack a tender person's attention and dig the already piercing shards of angst and shock in deeper and deeper. When people craft assumptive theories and presumptive conclusions from hearts inexperienced with deep grief, I can almost guarantee you two things:

- They fear dealing with their own covered-up places so much that they will spend their lives attempting to expose others.
- They don't have tan feet.

I spent quite a bit of time during this summer of being exposed thinking about how to deal with hurtful people. And I'll get to that in just a bit. But what I figured out I had to deal with first was my fear of other people's thoughts, opinions, whispers, and comments.

And after digging around in the Bible, I was surprised where God wanted me to start. Not with them. But with me. Not with their words. But with my fear.

After all, I will never be able to control what other people have going on in their heads or in their conversations. But with the help of the Holy Spirit in me, I can absolutely learn to control how much I allow the fear of their opinions to have access to my life. And working on something in my own heart has a much greater chance of getting traction. The more I focus on wanting others to change, the more frustrated I will become. But frustration can turn into forward motion when I take on the project of me.

My fears.

My worries based in fear.

And my anxiety bathed in fear.

Me and my tan feet decided to tackle a list of small fears first. I figured tackling big things like anxiety and worry was like trying to manually inflate a pool float the size of Kansas. It can be done, but you'd probably pass out and then quit way before you even see a smidge of progress. But child-size beach balls? They are doable, even for the average lung.

So, I decided to think of something I greatly feared but that would be doable to conquer today.

A two-piece bathing suit.

Jesus, take the wheel.

I cannot do that. I don't even think a two-piece bathing suit lines up with my theology. Or biology. And certainly not my forty-eight-year-old anatomy. No way. No how.

With eyes wide and forehead lines deeply carved into my expression, I willed myself to drive to the store. There was a ridiculous selection of strings with slight triangles sewn together to form most all the bottoms and the tops. I felt very certain this was the dumbest idea to have emerged in the history of all my thoughts ever.

But I knew this had absolutely nothing at all to do with a bathing suit. It had absolutely nothing to do with theology or biology or anatomy. It had everything to do with doing something in the physical that would give me eyes to see what was happening in the spiritual. Fear isn't something you can sweep up into a pile and discard. It isn't physical. It hovers and haunts us in the spiritual realm. It attacks us in the unseen. So bringing it out in plain sight in the form of a two-piece bathing suit helped me to touch it. Grasp it. And infuse just enough holy grit into my soul to pick the most conservative but still completely dangerous suit from a bottom sales rack and declare battle.

I kept mentally proclaiming over and over that this spirit of fear is not from God (2 Timothy 1:7). Therefore, it had to be coming from my enemy. As I put the suit on the cashier's conveyer belt. As I swung the plastic bag into the front passenger seat of my car. As I drove home feeling this strange and unfamiliar courage welling up from very deep within. As I popped the tags off. As I tugged it on and tied it up. As I stood there, completely alone in the privacy of my bedroom, facing the hardest step of all, turning to face myself in the mirror.

And that's where the fear intensified to the most painful level yet. I had to face myself if I was ever going to face this fear.

The enemy wants us paralyzed and compromised by the whispers and doubts and what-ifs and opinions and accusations and misunderstandings and all the other hissing handcuffs crafted by fear.

Standing there, feeling completely terrified to turn toward the mirror, it hit me. What gives power to all that I fear others are thinking and accusing and saying isn't the people themselves. It

The *enemy* wants us paralyzed and compromised by what-ifs, opinions, accusations, and misunderstandings.

isn't even the enemy. I'm the one who decides if their statements have power over me or not. It's me. And my desperate desire to stay covered up. I don't want to feel naked in any way. Even though I was technically in a bathing suit, I still felt so exposed. And I don't want to stand exposed, because I don't know how to do it and feel unashamed.

There it is. The root of this fear. I have allowed myself to believe that to be stripped of all the props and pretensions and accolades and approvals is to be stripped of the best parts of me. When in reality what's best about me comes to the forefront when I'm closest to the way God created me, naked and unashamed.

To stand naked and unashamed is the way of the garden life. "Adam and his wife were both naked, and they felt no shame" (Genesis 2:25).

Adam and Eve could do this, because they had no other opinions to contend with but the absolute love of God Himself. So there they stood before the Great Creator, whose heart exploded into a million hopes and dreams and purposes for these two vulnerable but valuable creatures before Him. His delight. His creation. His reflection.

Naked. Unashamed. And, therefore, completely unafraid.

For me, to turn and stand before myself this way was a marked moment of my casting off fear. It was my return to garden thinking. That garden reality that I can stand naked with no other opinion to contend with but the absolute love of God Himself. To dwell well in this life between two gardens requires one to make peace with being naked and unashamed. Not necessarily for the world to see. But just me and God.

I clenched my fist and started remembering statements others had made. I needed to speak to those statements and remove their power from my life.

When my biological dad said, "I wish I'd never had children," my interpretation that gave this statement power to fuel my fears was "You aren't wanted."

When the girls in middle school said, "Loser Lysa," the fuel to my fear was "You aren't accepted."

When the boy I had a crush on said, "I just like being your friend," the fuel to my fear was "You aren't pretty enough."

When the other mom said, "Your child is the worst," the fuel to my fear was "Your kids are going to be as messed up as you."

And then came the most hurtful of the statements, when my husband told me he'd met someone else. The fuel to my fear was "All the worst things you've ever wondered about yourself are true."

So, there was no shortage of fuel to help the statements of others, those who knew me and those who just knew about me, travel right to the core of my vulnerabilities and insecurities. I feared their statements, because they simply gave voice to thoughts that already haunted me.

If someone says something about me that's not true, I should be able to pull a Taylor Swift and simply shake it off. If it's a ridiculous statement, then it should be like a bad smell that may make me cringe for a few seconds but then passes on by.

But if someone says something about me that I've already wondered about myself, I probably won't be able to discern if it's ridiculous or not. I'll invite that statement in and offer it something to drink and a cozy seat in the corner of my mind. And before I know it, it's moved in like a bad roommate I never intended to have.

A roommate who comes into my bedroom when I'm trying on a two-piece bathing suit and reminds me of all the reasons I should never turn toward the mirror. Her damning statement? "You'll hate what you see. You in your exposed form is shameful. You should be afraid of who you really are."

And, just like Adam and Eve, I want to run. I want to cover up. I hear God calling for me, but I'm afraid of being naked, so I hide.

But isn't it interesting what God said to Adam? He didn't ask about the sin. He didn't scold him. He didn't point out Adam's flaws and all that was now wrong in the world because he ate the forbidden fruit. God's first two statements to Adam were:

"Where are you?" (Genesis 3:9).

And "Who told you that you were naked?" (Genesis 3:11).

God wasn't unaware of the answers to these questions. But Adam was. God posed these questions for Adam to process what just happened through recollection, response, and ultimately repentance through confession.

But please read God's words within a symphony of compassion. There was tenderness in God's actions; therefore, I believe there was tenderness in His tone. Adam and Eve were afraid. That's why they hid from God, and that's why they grabbed fig leaves and covered themselves. But instead of blaming and shaming them, God traded their fig leaves for fur. He handmade garments of skin to cover them. This foreshadowed the shedding of Jesus' blood to cover our sin. God knew that day in the garden their sin would be covered by the blood of an animal, but one day it would be the blood of His Son dripping from a cross. His ultimate act of compassion was foreshadowed by this act of compassion. Yes, there were consequences—sin always comes as a packaged deal with consequences. But don't miss the tenderness God had for His children. And don't miss God's tenderness for you.

If we were together right now, I'd turn to you, with tears of true understanding, and whisper, "Who told you that you were naked? Who told you that you are anything less than a most glorious creation of the Almighty God? Who spoke words over you and about you that stripped you bare and broke your heart?"

Whatever statement was spoken to you that came against the truth **must be called a lie**!

God's Word is the Truth. And His Truth says you are a holy and dearly loved child of your heavenly Father.

You are wonderfully made.

You are a treasure.

You are beautiful.

You are fully known by Him and lavishly loved by Him.

You are chosen.

You are special.

You are set apart.

No matter what you've done or what's been done to you, these words of God are true about you.

May we carefully choose what we remember and what we forget.

I'm so quick to remember others' hurtful words but slow to remember God's healing words.

We must set our minds and our hearts on things above by choosing to remember God's words, repeat God's words, and believe God's words about us.

We must let God's Word become the words we park our minds and hearts on.

We must let God's Word become the words of our story.

We must let God's Word become the words we believe and receive as truth.

We must let God's Word become the words of our story.

I heard a symphony of compassion fill my bedroom. I heard God uninviting the hurtful statements and removing their power. *Who told you that? Aren't they broken, vulnerable people, with their own hurts and heartbreaks? Might you have compassion for them but not be overpowered by their thoughts? And might you have compassion for yourself? Who told you that you were naked? And who told you that you in your naked form are anything but glorious?*

I swallowed hard. And I turned toward the mirror.

I turned. And I didn't die. I didn't even cringe. There I was, fully exposed. My age evident. My flaws in full view. My surgery scar running like an exclamation point right down my middle. But I was standing. Strong. Maybe stronger than I'd ever been in my entire life.

I could almost feel fear losing its grip on me. Untangling its strangling effects so much I was almost inspired to go out in public. But then Jesus most certainly took the wheel and bossed me and my tan feet to just let this lesson sink in, down deep, to where it matters most, inside of this new, slightly unafraid me. Naked and unashamed. So deeply loved by God.

GOING *to the* WELL

When you live slow for a season, the Son has access to the parts of you normally covered up by everyday put-ons.

REMEMBER:

- I must learn to control how much I allow fear to have access to my life.
- The enemy wants us paralyzed and compromised by what-ifs, opinions, accusations, and misunderstandings.
- To dwell well in this life between two gardens requires us to make peace with being naked and unashamed.
- We must let God's Word become the words of our story.
- I am deeply loved by God, even in my most naked form.

RECEIVE:

Adam and his wife were both naked, and they felt no shame. (Genesis 2:25)

Also read:
Genesis 3:9, 11
2 Timothy 1:7

REFLECT:

- Whom have you given so much power to that their words about you being naked make you afraid? How have their words affected you?
- Have you ever feared dealing with your own covered-up places so much that you attempted to expose others instead? How has that played out?
- How are you living paralyzed by fear instead of in the reality that you are deeply loved by God?

Father,

I confess that I spend too much time mentally revisiting the hurtful words of others instead of purposefully reminding my soul of healing words from You. I come to You today with a soul that is tired. Tired of running. Tired of hiding. Tired of feeling like I'm never quite enough. Help me receive and believe the words that You say are true about me. That I am a treasure. That I am beautiful. That I am chosen and set apart. Even with all my flaws. Even with all these scars. Strip away every label, every lie, and even the masks I've desperately tried to hold in place, and help me simply stand before You today. Naked and unashamed. Fully known and lavishly loved.

In Jesus' name, amen.

PAINT

AND P

NGS
EOPLE

Chapter 5
PAINTINGS AND PEOPLE

*I*t was July 21. My forty-eighth birthday. I was in one of the hardest parts of this season of suffering. The season of dust. I wasn't able to do the typical "Hey, since this is my birthday, let me just do a little planning . . . a little dreaming" thing.

Nope. The future felt impossibly scary. I could only face the future in teaspoons of time. Not weeks and months and certainly not a whole year.

When there is an undoing of your life, there is an unknowing of every next millisecond. Every next breath. The peaceful predictability of what you thought would be your life is suddenly replaced by a very unexpected darkness and silence you aren't used to. It's like when the power suddenly goes out in an office with no windows. It's jolting. What was full of activity and productivity and plans and important details and bosses bossing and workers working becomes as quiet as a hospice hallway.

Darkness has such a way of swallowing up enthusiasm for the future.

No, this birthday would not be about looking at the year ahead and dreaming up how to build upon the previous forty-seven. Not when a blackout of epic proportions had just spilled out across the pages of all my hopes and dreams and assumptions of how safe tomorrow would surely be.

Year forty-eight for me was supposed to be the year of the last of our five kids going to college. A year of empty-nest bonding. No more carpool schedules or parent-teacher meetings on a Tuesday night. Those things were all part of the glorious season of growing a family. But now we could be carefree and plan a date on a Tuesday. A long walk on a Wednesday. And then really go crazy and decide on a Friday morning to just drive to the mountains or the beach.

The pages of our life were going to be as fun and predictable as one of those beautiful adult coloring books. Twenty-five years of marriage had helped life take shape, so all we had to do now was just add color. Coloring in what is already beautifully drawn is predictably fun for me. There's no stress when your highest risk is whether to color the flowers purple or yellow or pink.

But on this forty-eighth birthday I opened the coloring book, and someone had erased all the beautifully drawn lines.

There was nothing but white pages. Empty spaces. Endless possibilities of fear and failure.

Metaphorically speaking, my life was now a blank canvas.

I think I shared this feeling with my mother. And you know what she did? She suggested—no, actually she demanded—we get some blank canvases and paint on my birthday. She wanted us to drive to the arts and craft store (#hives) and survive brushing shoulders with real artists. They would all know I was a craft-store imposter. An eye-roller at glue guns. A cringer at all things glittery and gooey. A passerby of the paintbrush.

Which, by the way, I quickly learned came in approximately 467 options unbudding artists like me can stress over after we enter said craft store, not to mention all the different kinds of paint. And then there were the zillions of color options that made me want to just lie down in the middle of the aisle and take a nap. Can you imagine my mom trying to explain to all the real artists why her forty-eight-year-old daughter was in such a state?

Thank heavens the craft store was slow that day. So, the apron-wearing sales gal with pigtails, pep, and painting knowledge had time to help us.

We loaded up on supplies and headed home.

As we were driving I kept reminding myself that this was going to be good and fun and that there was no pressure to perform or do this painting thing perfectly. I was with my mother, who has always had an overly enthusiastic response to anything I've ever tried. She would love whatever spilled out onto my canvas. This is the woman who heard me give a book report in elementary school and decided I should be the first woman president of the United States. Bless her heart.

She is also the one who once loved a little story I wrote so much that she wanted me to call Willie Nelson and have him write a song to go with it. Willie. Nelson. Because I'm sure Willie is sitting by the phone today, waiting for a strange girl with craft-store hives to offer him some assistance with his musical career. And then, wait for it, she also wanted me to **offer to sing it with him.**

Ask me if I sing.

No.

Nor do I paint.

But I promise you right there, in my little car loaded down with craft supplies, said mom of mine was making plans in her head about which museum would surely need my first painting more: the Metropolitan Museum in New York or the National Gallery in Washington, DC. No one has ever told her that some pieces of art are fit for a mom's corkboard, not a gallery display.

I love her enthusiasm. Until it's directed at me while I'm holding a dripping, shaking paintbrush.

My sisters joined us, which helped divvy up Mom's enthusiasm.

I painted a boat. They all painted angels.

And while my mom was right—it was therapeutic in many ways—it was also a terrifyingly vulnerable experience.

It was my moment to be the painter instead of the observer. It was my moment to face disappointment from the angle of an artist. And to be the painter I would both display my ability but even more scary expose my inability. I came across a quote from the book *Art and Fear* that says it best: "Making art provides uncomfortably accurate feedback about the gap that inevitably exists between what you intended to do, and what you did."[3] And the gap never stays silent. It reverberates with commentary. Sadly, for too many of us it's a negative commentary. This is such a ploy of Satan. He loves to take a beautiful moment of life and fill it with a negative narrative about our failures that plays over and over until the voice of God is hushed. Satan perverts the reality that we are beloved children of God. He wants our thoughts to be tightly entangled in his thoughts.

These are his thoughts. This is his script: *Not. Good. Enough.* We hear it when we try to create. We hear it when we try to be brave and start anything new. We hear it when we try to overcome what has been and step into what could be.

Remember, while God converts with truth, the enemy perverts the truth. God wants us transformed, but Satan wants us paralyzed. So when we hear thoughts like *I'm not good enough* that cause us to shrink away, we must keep in mind that the enemy will do anything he can to prevent us from moving closer to God or connecting more deeply with other people. This "truth" we think we hear is not truth at all. In chapter 9, we'll talk

> While God converts with truth, the enemy perverts the truth.

more about the three ways the enemy attacks us. But for now, rest assured, God wants us near, no matter our imperfections.

The enemy of my soul didn't want me painting that day. To create meant that I would look a little bit like my Creator. To overcome the terrifying angst of the blank canvas meant I would forever have more compassion for other artists. You better believe as I placed the first blue and gray strokes onto the white emptiness before me, the "not good enough" statement was pulsing through my head in almost deafening tones.

And please make note that the enemy doesn't leave this "not good enough" script as a general whisper that passes through our thoughts. No, he makes it very personal. So personal, in fact, we determine it's an authentic assessment of mounting evidence that we fall so very short. We don't even know this is all coming from the enemy, because the recognizable voice we hear saying it over and over is our own.

I am not good enough.

How recently have you had this thought about yourself?

Maybe yours wasn't with a paintbrush in hand. But I know you've felt it too. Anytime you feel disappointed in yourself, the enemy will cue this script.

This paralyzing lie is one of his favorite tactics to keep you disillusioned by disappointments. Walls go up, emotions run high, we get guarded, defensive, demotivated, and paralyzed by the endless ways we feel doomed to fail. This is when we quit. This is when we put the kids in front of the TV because nothing in the parenting books seems to be working. This is when we settle for the ease of Facebook instead of the more challenging work of digging into God's book of transformation. This is when we get a job to simply make money instead of pursuing our calling to make a difference. This is when we coast in our relationships rather than investing in true intimacy. This is when we put the paintbrush down and don't even try.

So there I was. Standing before my painted blue boat, making the choice of which voice to listen to.

I'm convinced God was smiling. Pleased. Asking me to find delight in what is right. Wanting me to have compassion for myself by focusing on that part of my painting that expressed something beautiful. To just be eager to give that beauty to whoever dared to look at my boat. To create to love others. Not to beg them for validation.

But the enemy was perverting all that. Perfection mocked my boat. The bow was too high, the details too elementary, the reflection on the water too abrupt, and the back of the boat too off-center. Disappointment demanded I hyper-focus on what didn't look quite right.

It was my choice which narrative to hold on to: "Not good enough" or "Find delight in what is right." Each perspective swirled, begging me to declare it as truth.

I was struggling to make peace with my painting creation, because I was struggling to make peace with myself as God's creation. Anytime we feel not good enough we deny the powerful truth that we are a glorious work of God in progress.

We are imperfect because we are unfinished.

So, as unfinished creations, of course everything we touch will have imperfections. Everything we attempt will have imperfections. Everything we accomplish will have imperfections. And that's when it hit me: I expect a perfection in me and a perfection in others that not even God Himself expects. If God is patient with the process, why can't I be?

How many times have I let imperfections cause me to be too hard on myself and too harsh with others?

I forced myself to send a picture of my boat to at least twenty friends. With each text I sent, I was slowly making peace with my painting's imperfections. I was determined to not be held back by the enemy's accusations that my artwork wasn't good enough to be considered "real art." Again, this wasn't for validation but rather confirmation that I could see the imperfections in my painting but not deem it worthless. I could see the imperfections in me and not deem myself worthless. It was an act of self-compassion.

We must get to this place of self-compassion if we ever hope to have true, deep compassion for others. Disappointment begs

We are

imperfect

because we are

unfinished.

us to be secretly disgusted with everything and everyone who has gaps, everything and everyone who also wrestles with the "not good enough" script. But what if, instead of being so epically disappointed with everyone, we saw in them the need for compassion? The artist, the writer, the preacher, the prostitute, the teacher, the ones who run carpools, the ones who run races, the wives, the husbands, the singles, the coworkers, the teenagers, the small children, the larger-than-life superstars, the ones on top of the world, and the forgotten ones at rock bottom. No exceptions. They all need compassion.

This is a much bigger deal than I'd ever known before my season of sorrow. On the surface there doesn't seem much danger in not having compassion for others. But make no mistake, a lack of compassionate connection with our fellow humans is part of a much bigger move of the enemy.

If he can distract us with the negative narrative of "not good enough," we will miss the metanarrative, the grand overarching story of redemption in which God intends for us all to play a crucial role. Understand that no time showing up and bringing compassion to another human is ever a waste of time. Rather, it's our chance to bring context, purpose, and meaning to all of life. Quiet moments of compassion are epic moments of battle. They happen when we hush the chaos and shame of Satan with the truth of Revelation 12:11: "They triumphed over him by the blood of the Lamb and by the word of their testimony." Jesus has brought the blood. We must bring the word of our testimony.

We are most triumphant when we place our disappointments in God's hands and say, "Lord, I trust You to redeem this and return it to me as part of my testimony." Our disappointments in ourselves—in our lives—aren't just isolated pieces of evidence that we fall short and life is hard. No, they are the exact places where we can break secrecy with fellow humans and show up to say, "Me too. I get it. I understand. You aren't alone. Together, we can find our way home."

Just as breaking bread with another hungry human feeds our bodies with nourishment, breaking secrecy with another hurting human feeds our souls with compassion. We take the comfort of God we've received in the midst of our disappointments and use it to bring comfort to others. In the words of the apostle Paul, "Praise be to the God and Father of our Lord Jesus Christ, the Father of compassion and the God of all comfort, who comforts us in all our troubles, so that we can comfort those in any trouble with the comfort we ourselves receive from God" (2 Corinthians 1:3–4).

When we show up with compassion for others, our own disappointments won't ring as hollow or sting with sorrow nearly as much.

A few weeks into my painting adventure, my house was filled with canvases. And I decided it was time to go to an art show to look at other people's work. Now that I dared to be a painter, I felt I could break secrecy with another painter. I knew her terror, her angst, her disappointment, her wondering if she was good enough. She didn't need to worry about keeping all that a secret, because I wouldn't require her paintings to live up to any unrealistic expectations. I would bring compassion.

I now knew to stand before each painting with nothing but

When we show up with compassion for others, our own disappointments won't ring as hollow or sting with sorrow nearly as much.

love, amazement, and delight. I refused to demand anything more from the artist. I just wanted to show up for every single piece she was so brave to put on display. I fought against any negative thought as if I were fighting away a hound of hell from taking even the slightest bit of ground.

Might I just be courageous enough to stand before her work and require myself to find everything about it I love? Release my clenched fist and pouty disappointments, and trade my "live up" mentality for a "show up" one? It's so much more freeing to simply show up and be a finder of the good. Break from the secret disappointments. Let my brain venture down the tiny little opening of love. A sliver of light sweetness in this world wrought with dark judgments, disgruntled comments, jagged-edged opinions, and lofty huffs of disgust.

As I took in painting after painting at that art show, I showed up.

And, finally, I realized what makes paintings so delightful. It's their imperfections. We already know a painting isn't going to look like a photograph. And that's what makes it art. It's been touched by a human. It's been created by someone whose hands sweat and who can't possibly transfer divine perfection from what her corneas see to what her fingertips can create.

Even the best painters will get something off scale, out of alignment, a shade too dark, or a hair too thick. It will be flawed. And that's where we must make a crucial decision: What will we do with disappointment?

Will we see it as an unraveling of the precision we long for? A mockery of perfection? An unbecoming? Another disappointment to add to all the other disappointments we constantly feel?

Or, will we see the human behind the ink? The heart that dared to hold the brush dripping with color. Remember that she was the courageous one. That she was the one who showed up. Took the risk. Braved the secret disappointments of others. And lived. And made her mark.

I love her for doing that.

And, therefore, I can love her work.

We dare to have affection for a painting not because of our tolerance of it but because of our delight in the way it carries its imperfections. It's personally unique. It eloquently expresses something our souls understand in the unseen connection we make when we stand before it.

There is a burst of courage that will explode off the canvas if we don't shrink back afraid. The moment the painter laid down her brush and stepped back, pleased, is when she allowed that painting to steal a few beats of her very own heart for you. The viewer. Close your eyes and receive this very human gift without any demand for more or better. And just show up and live.

The way we show up for a painting is a direct reflection of the way we will show up for people.

Regardless of who they are and how they are, there is only one way to stand before paintings and people. With compassion. That doesn't mean you agree with everything they say or everything they do. But it does mean you value each of them as a person. A person who needs compassion.

I like that word *compassion*. It's being aware that all of us fear the imperfections deeply carved into our naked selves. We all cover up. And then we all get stripped bare when the wins become losses. Who do you want standing near you in those moments dripping with disappointment and saturated with sorrow? I can assure you it isn't people who don't know the whole story, draped in gold-plated pride with mouths eager to spill out commentary like, "Here's what you did wrong. I would never have allowed myself to get in this position. If only you would have . . ."

Nope. It's those clothed with garments of understanding. They have personally experienced that this life between two gardens can sometimes make it excruciatingly painful to simply be human. They keep in mind the Bible's instructions, as we rub shoulders human to human. "Therefore, as God's chosen people, holy and dearly loved, clothe yourselves with compassion, kindness, humility, gentleness and patience" (Colossians 3:12).

We are to put on each of these things every day like a painter puts on color he knows will connect his creation with others. God wants you, His creation, to connect with others and bring them light and life with the brush strokes of compassion. Note that compassion is listed first in Colossians 3:12. It's from a heart of compassion that kindness, humility, gentleness, and patience naturally flow. Just as the best paintings have the most distinct focal point, God wants you and me, His favorite creations, to have the focal point of compassion.

When people see us, do they see the compassion of their Creator?

If so, I guarantee when the enemy sees us he shakes with fear. He isn't scared of the judgmental soul shellacked with a fake sense of perfection. But the compassionate soul who has hurt deeply and come out loving? Yes, she is one of the superstars of God's grand story, and the one you want near you in the battles of life.

She wears well the scars of suffering and can't wait to tell you her survival story so you, too, can survive. She has great compassion toward every created thing, whether it be covered in paint or flesh or dust.

The only way to gain more of this compassion is to pick up a paintbrush for yourself and sit in the seat of your own suffering.

If you have ever experienced an unexpected darkness, a silence and stillness you aren't used to, know that these hard times, these devastating disappointments, these seasons of suffering are not for nothing. They will grow you. They will shape you. They will soften you. They will allow you to experience God's comfort and compassion. But you will find life-giving purpose and meaning when you allow God to take your painful experiences and comfort others. You will be able to share a unique hope because you know exactly what it feels like to be them.

In my own season of suffering I feel as though I've licked the floor of hell. So now everything else in comparison looks a little more heavenly. I promise. I know. Paintings and people are more beautiful to me than I've ever before troubled myself to see. Paintings and people need the compassion I've now gained. Paintings and people need the more hopeful outlook I can now bring. Now it's your turn—hurting one, become a helping one.

Pick up the paintbrush. Feel the tension. Feel the fear and weight of every view, all the eyes, all the opinions. Choose to be converted by showing up with God's life-giving truth, not perverted by the enemy's death blows of discouragement. Let your heart beat fast and furious and wild and terrified. Drumming against your chest and begging you to get on beat with Him.

Show up.

People need you. People need me. People need to know God's compassion is alive and well and winning the epic battle of good versus evil. People need to know redemption is more than just a word.

Put some paint on the emptiness. Color-correct your perspective. Forget the cravings for comfort zones. Trade your comfort for compassion. Don't welcome hardness of heart as easiness of life. Get wet with paint. Put the brush to the canvas. Own it. Declare yourself a painter. And when someone steals all the lines from your coloring book, determine to color the world anyhow with the same generosity of compassion that God offers every day.

Be like Him. The Creator, the Master Artist.

Don't be like them. The hard-hearted haters. The ones who refuse to admit that their coloring books are missing lines too. The ones who refuse to break secrets with their fellow humans. The ones who would rather criticize than comfort. The ones who are loud with their opinions but who have never suffered with a blank canvas.

Grab the brush, and light the world with your color and attempts at creation. Don't try to be perfect. Don't pretend it's even possible. Don't apologize or strategize. And don't minimize that you are crushing fear and judgment with every stroke. You are walking the way of the artist. You are simply showing up with compassion. And I love you for that. I love whatever is about to come to life on your canvas to the glory of our Almighty Creator. God. The Redeemer of dust. The Redeemer of us.

Well, cue the Willie Nelson song, Mom. And let's paint and sing together until the forty-eight candles burn out.

GOING *to the* WELL

We are imperfect because we are unfinished.

REMEMBER:

- While God converts with Truth, the enemy perverts the Truth.
- God wants us transformed, but Satan wants us paralyzed.
- To create means that I look a little bit like my Creator.
- God doesn't expect perfection, so we shouldn't expect it from ourselves and others.
- We must get to a place of self-compassion if we hope to ever have true, deep compassion for others.
- Quiet moments of compassion are epic moments of battle.
- We must trade our "live up" mentality for a "show up" one.
- People need to know God's compassion is alive and well and winning the epic battle of good versus evil.

RECEIVE:

Praise be to the God and Father of our Lord Jesus Christ, the Father of compassion and the God of all comfort, who comforts us in all our troubles, so that we can comfort those in any trouble with the comfort we ourselves receive from God. (2 Corinthians 1:3–4)

Also read:
Colossians 3:12
Revelation 12:11

REFLECT:

- When people see you, do they see the compassion of their Creator? How so?
- How many times have you let imperfections cause you to be too hard on yourself and too harsh with others?
- What might it look like in your daily life for you to bring compassion as you show up for others?

Father,

I don't want to let disappointment and heartbreak cause me to approach this life more cautious than creative. More critical than compassionate. More cynical than surrendered. Thank You for the ways You tenderly meet me in my brokenness and my pain. And thank You for reminding me that I still have light and beauty to offer to this world. Today, I am choosing to grab the brush. No attempts at perfection. No apologizing or strategizing. Just me. Lighting this world with my color. Showing up with Your compassion and grace.

In Jesus' name, amen.

A LITTL

LONG A

LOT TO

Chapter 6

A LITTLE TOO LONG AND
A LOT TOO HARD

I think it's important to note at this point in the book that I don't know when or how my circumstances are going to be restored.

Sometimes, you just have to let people you love have their journey on one side of the street and have yours on the other side of the street.

Our counselors are wise, and we listen to them. They know how to do this. We don't. So, during this part of the journey, Art doesn't live with me. There's not one part of me that likes this or wants this. But this is reality.

I come home many nights to a very quiet house. Our kids are grown and they visit often, but then, when family get-togethers end, everyone leaves. Including Art. I can't describe the pain of watching him walk down our front sidewalk and then drive away. Our house used to be crazy-loud and full of activity but is now as still as an evacuated town. The thrashing winds of the storm are gone, but the consequences make it impossible to return to something that feels normal. We make brief visits to normal, but there's a lot of emotional debris to which we must tend. Little by little, we make progress in the two-steps-forward-one-step-back kind of way. But when the lights go out, I'm alone.

A soul-shaking silence and disappointment about my current situation is what goes to bed with me in the dark. And it's what's there with me in the middle of the night when I've had another nightmare. And this reality is still there each time my eyes open to the next new day. And the next. And the next.

I don't say this to invite you into any sort of pity party but to say I understand how hard it is when deep disappointments linger on and on. You probably have middle-of-the-night moments of wrestling through your own tears.

The glaring disappointment of negative pregnancy tests month after month while your closest friends are decorating their soon-to-be-filled nurseries.

The emptiness in your heart because that person you love doesn't seek to really understand you, rarely cheers you on, and doesn't seem to want to connect intimately with you.

The draining frustration of never being the one chosen for the job or ministry opportunity you've dreamed about for a long, long time.

The excruciating fear of watching your kids make poor choices no matter how hard you pray for them.

The heartbreak of that friendship that fell apart despite your best efforts to hold it together.

The painful symptoms of a chronic illness that leave you feeling weak, frustrated, and misunderstood.

The weight of living with so much financial debt that you can't enjoy your life or the people in it.

And in your most private moments you want to scream words you don't use around your Bible friends at the unfairness of it all. You, too, have memories that still hurt. Realities that make you swallow back tears. Heartache that pumps sorrow through your veins. Sufferings that seem forever long. And you're disappointed that today you aren't living the promises of God you've begged to come to pass. You're tired of this disappointment lingering a little too long and being a bit too hard.

When things stay hard for a long time, every day feels more like walking on a tightrope than on a solid and secure road into the future.

I'm balancing on that tightrope. I'm no longer at the first cliff where the ground fell out from beneath me. But I'm also not all the way across to solid ground where everyone exhales, exhausted but relieved. No, I'm in the middle, which honestly might be the scariest of all places.

Moving ahead and turning back are both equally terrifying.

My feet are shaky. My ankles twitch like they are going to turn, and then I'll surely fall off this tightrope I find myself on.

Tears stream down my face as I try to find my balance. "God, I feel like I'm dying. Do You care? Are You there? How in the world can I reconcile the fact that You say You love me but then You leave me here? In this middle place."

Surely my cries for help will prompt God to make it better. But then, out of nowhere, I start to get assaulted by fire-tipped darts flying at me and piercing my already bleeding soul. On top of my devastating marriage circumstances comes a major issue with mold under the house. And then the city notifies us that they are widening the road in front of our house, requiring that we move our driveway so they can also put in a turn lane. Ask me if they are paying for this. No. Then my grown kids seem to take turns having their own crisis situations. And finally, I get a call from my doctor that something showed up on my latest mammogram that he didn't like. More tests need to be done. One of these situations a year would be a lot on its own. But having them happening constantly, day after day, feels cruel.

I came home today and sat on my bed, that quiet place where I feel most safe and most terrified all at once.

It felt like too much.

It was too hard.

These days, I'm not sure if I'm standing on a tightrope, just trying to make it to the other side, or walking a plank of death. Seriously. I'm not being dramatic.

And neither are you. If you identify with any of this, you get it.

The sun is going down. Darkness is on its way. The tightrope is swaying, hope is fading, and gravity is screaming that I'll fall . . . or fall apart. Either way, it all makes me afraid to exhale.

I ask a question I've sworn I wouldn't ask. But I can no longer keep it at bay. *Why me?*

Sometimes all the homes around me seem to be bursting with laughter and love and a normalcy currently out of reach for me. I'm happy for them. I used to be one of them. But it's so hard to see the stark contrast of their lives and mine. We all have areas of life that seem to fall impossibly short. We thought this aspect of life would bring us great joy. After all, it does for others. But not us. The very thing we thought would burn so brightly with joy has turned out to burn us.

And what makes it so maddening is that it didn't have to be this way! Usually, the most disappointing realities come from the most realistic expectations. An unmet longing from a realistic expectation is such a searing pain within a human heart. You know this whole deal should have and could have been different. But their choices were their own. Their desires, their brokenness, their selfishness, or their lack of awareness left your needs unattended. What seemed so realistic to you was met with a resistance and ultimately a rejection by someone you didn't think would ever hurt you.

I'm not a fan of the pity party's rallying cry, *why me?* But it sure is understandable in these cases.

One minute I want to spit and stomp and slam my fist down on my table with no dinner—no people—no normalcy. The next I want to crank up the praise music and pull out a fresh canvas to paint. I read a note sent by a friend whose ink is smeared with the sweat of her own struggle. She makes me feel not so alone for a few minutes. But the sun still goes down that night. The darkness envelops my quiet house. And my husband won't be there to stick my cold feet under when I go to bed or to whisper "You're not alone. At least we have each other. We'll get through this together." No matter how much my heart needs those words right now . . . those needs won't be met tonight. Maybe one day, but not today.

And that's what it is like to be so very human—hurting but still hoping.

Hoping doesn't mean I put myself in harm's way. It doesn't mean I ignore reality. No, hoping means I acknowledge reality in the very same breath that I acknowledge God's sovereignty.

And, I've learned one more important fact: my hope isn't tied to my expectations finally being met in my way and in my timing. No. My hope isn't tied to whether or not a circumstance or another person changes. My hope is tied to the unchanging promise of God. I hope for the good I know God will ultimately bring from this, whether the good turns out to match my desires or not.

My hope is tied to the unchanging promise of God.

And, sometimes, that takes a while. Remember what we talked about a few chapters back. God loves us too much to answer our prayers in any other way than the right way. And He loves us too much to answer our prayers at any other time than the right time.

The process will most likely require us to be persevering. Patient. Maybe even longsuffering.

Longsuffering. It's not a word I want to be part of my story. But as my friends have prayed for me, this word keeps bubbling up. Longsuffering means having or showing patience despite troubles, especially those caused by other people.

Hello, God? Can I make some suggestions of really saintly people who would handle being longsuffering much better than I would? Remember, I'm the girl who is completely terrified of this whole deal. I want these devastating disappointments to go away today. I don't want this suffering to last this long. It's already been nearly three years. And I'm just so very tired.

I pray—no, I beg—for things to change soon. And maybe they will by the time this book goes to print. But maybe they won't.

And that's why I feel compelled to write this chapter from a very uncertain, untidy place. I know I must walk through God's process before I see His fulfilled promise. I think I already said that in a previous chapter, but it's worth repeating when my mind keeps forgetting.

And maybe you need to remember that too. Regardless of whether your longsuffering is because of something big or small, remember pain is pain. It's all relative in the scope of your own life. And God's promises aren't just for certain people at a certain low point. His hope extends into any and every size pit or pothole. Please don't think if your situation isn't catastrophic that you shouldn't bring it to our discussion here. Sweet sister, pull up a chair and pull out your journaled heartbreaks, and I'll do the same. My disappointment needs a promise fulfilled, and so does yours.

You need to be tenderly cared for, and so do I. We need each other. We need to remind each other that we will eventually get to a better place.

It's hard to remember what solid ground feels like when you're shaking in the middle of the tightrope.

I'm desperate to see a promise fulfilled right now. I want God to magically make a bridge appear around the tightrope, so I don't have to walk so slowly and be so scared as I make my way to the other side of all this.

I want the promised blessing of Psalm 40:4: "Blessed is the one who trusts in the Lord." I forget that this kind of trusting in God is often forged in the crucible of longsuffering. God isn't picking on me. God is picking me to personally live out one of His promises.

I know I must walk

through God's

process before I

see His fulfilled

promise.

It's a high honor. But it doesn't always feel that way.

I've got to walk through the low places of the process before I'm perfectly equipped to live the promise.

We read about some of the low places of the process in verses 1–3 of Psalm 40:

> I waited patiently for the LORD;
>> he turned to me and heard my cry.
> He lifted me out of the slimy pit,
>> out of the mud and mire;
> he set my feet on a rock
>> and gave me a firm place to stand.
> He put a new song in my mouth,
>> a hymn of praise to our God.
> Many will see and fear the LORD
>> and put their trust in him.

I want the solid rock on which to stand, but first I have to wait patiently for the Lord to lift me out of the slime and mud and set my feet. That word *set* in the original Hebrew is *qum*, which means to arise or take a stand. God has to take me through the process of getting unstuck from what's been holding me captive before I can take a stand.

I also want that new song promised here. Did you notice, though, what comes before the psalm's promise of a new song? It's the many cries to the Lord for help. The most powerful praise songs don't start out as beautiful melodies; rather, they start as guttural cries of pain. But soon the process of pain turns into the promise of a praise like no other.

Keep walking the tightrope, Lysa. One foot in front of the

other. Catch your breath when necessary, but don't stop. Not today. Not tomorrow. Jesus is here, and He will not let you fall.

Don't miss this. We've talked about the process on the way to the promise. But we must not forget His presence in the midst of the process.

The promise is a glorious hope to hang on to for the future. But it's His presence in the process that will steady our hope for today.

I swallow hard. I put some Visine in my very red eyes. I remind myself to breathe. I know He's placed people and things around me with great intentionality to assure me I'm not alone on this tightrope journey.

So, I look around for evidence of His presence. I find the first thing. It's a little blue-and-white booklet.

Ironically, my ministry is knee-deep in a study of the book of Job right now. The daily experience guide we print for the participants of our study is right here with me. It's called "Suffering and Sovereignty." And I know this isn't irony; God had it well planned.

I feel like Job.

The Lord was with him. But everything about his circumstances begged him to no longer be with the Lord. And here's what I imagine would have been the hardest part about being Job: being completely uncertain of the outcome. We read the book of Job in the context of knowing the restoration that comes at the end. It helps us not feel the true intensity of Job's pain.

And while I know in my head that God will somehow, someday turn all this around for good in my life, too, my heart isn't so sure some moments. The intensity of the pain gives me a propensity to doubt.

God, give me relief from my unbelief!

I flip to the part of the little blue-and-white book that reveals the end of Job's story. And I open my Bible to all the scriptures listed. I borrow his good ending. I tuck it into my heart. I preach these scriptures of hope to myself over and over.

> After Job had prayed for his friends [the ones who misjudged Job, didn't tell the truth about God, and added so much hurt on top of Job's pain] the LORD restored his fortunes and gave him twice as much as he had before. (Job 42:10)

> The LORD blessed the latter part of Job's life more than the former part. (Job 42:12)

> Job lived a hundred and forty years; he saw his children and their children to the fourth generation. (Job 42:16)

God put Job's story here to help guide me through the process of my story. And God put that blue-and-white book here today, reminding me to look at Job's story as evidence of His presence in my process. I know it.

If I were you right now, I'd be like, *Okay, I don't see a little blue-and-white book, so how do I know God's presence is here for me personally?* Well, I pray my book, the one you're holding in your hand, is one of those things. God made sure this message got to you in the middle of whatever you are facing right now.

But there are other evidences of His presence around us. I promise.

God is in often overlooked places. We don't have to find Him. God is not far from us.

We just have to make the choice to see Him and rightly attribute to Him the good that does exist. I truly believe what keeps us on the path of longsuffering instead of veering off in the dangerous direction of wallowing is to wake up with great expectation of these little reminders of God's goodness.

A few days later I look around again.

In the darkness of my quiet room, I move a stack of papers and a few unread books. Underneath is a small white pouch. It doesn't make sense that this white pouch is here. I'm clueless how it found its way under this stack. I always keep it with my jewelry. It is the most valuable piece of metal in my possession, so I'm never careless with it. I would never have put it there.

But there it is.

Hello, God.

Inside there's a gold and purple medal. I haven't thought about it in a while. But in this moment I feel that if I don't pull it out and press it into my hand I will not be able to steady myself. Hard realities are slamming into me once again. So finding this gift on this day in this moment is perfect.

I exhale and know God is here. Again.

I'm reminded of the time I received this gift.

It is on loan from my counselor. A real purple heart. The high honor the government had given to his family when his brother-in-law was killed in the line of duty trying to save others.

This counselor had been working with my husband and me slow and steady for the better part of a year. We've spent more than seventy-five hours in his office. We flew out to Colorado for five separate weeklong intensives. It was all with the understanding that we were on the same page and moving ahead together. All the devastation would be repaired and restored and made right.

But during one of our last sessions, I think my counselor knew something was not right. And I think he felt we were going to leave his office and walk into one of the fiercest seasons of this battle. He took the professionally done frame off his office wall and tore the backing to open it. He pulled out this priceless medal. He knelt in front of us and placed it in my hand.

"Hold on to this, Lysa, for as long as you need it. When the battle gets so fierce you wonder if you will survive, remember this moment of my telling you that you will make it through this. If God gave out purple hearts, you would absolutely receive this high honor. What you are going through won't be for nothing. Your hurt will not be wasted. It will be for the saving of many lives."

I looked down at this ridiculously outrageous gift, speechless. The moment stole all my words, and I had nothing to offer back to him but tears. I mouthed the words "thank you." I felt brave that day.

Less than a month after we returned home from that counseling appointment, my heart was devastated again.

I couldn't breathe. The medal was the only physical thing I felt I could hold on to when every bit of my life was flying around as shattered debris. I had thought we were almost done with this horrific season, and then I realized we hadn't even started the healing. What I thought was a miracle in the making was actually setting me up to be caught off guard and deeply wounded again.

Years of this kind of hurt have taken quite a toll. The memories linger. They pierce tender places deep within.

And now, on this day, I find the medal again. The purple heart can't heal me, but it sure does steady me. So, even with a limp, I can take one more step across the tightrope. Just one more step is all I need to take today. And I can take this step because I'm assured of His presence in the process.

And not only is His presence in the process, but there's also a purpose in the process.

Longsuffering is long because you can't sprint through it. It's one step. And then another that might be more treacherous than all the previous steps. Getting to that solid rock from Psalm 40 might require a bit of a hike. Sometimes God lifts us up in an instant, and other times He wants to join us on a bit of a journey—a process through which we can gain a little more strength and grit and lung capacity for what He sees we'll need once we reach that rock at the top. There is a purpose to the process, and it's called preparation.

The process isn't a cruel way to keep you from the promise; it's the exact preparation you'll need to handle the promise.

If God thought we could handle the promise today, He'd lift us up today. But if we aren't standing on that firm rock, singing a glorious song, it's because He loves us too much to lift us up there right now. This process isn't a cruel way to keep you from the promise; it's the exact preparation you'll need to handle the promise.

So many Bible verses speak to this process that produces what we will need when we step into the promise. Here are some of my favorites:

> And the God of all grace, who called you to his eternal glory in Christ, after you have suffered a little while, will himself restore you and make you strong, firm and steadfast. (1 Peter 5:10)

> For this reason, since the day we heard about you, we have not stopped praying for you. We continually ask God to fill you with the knowledge of his will through all the wisdom and under-standing that the Spirit gives, so that you may live a life worthy of the Lord and please him in every way: bearing fruit in every good work, growing in the knowledge of God, being strengthened with

all power according to his glorious might so that you may have great endurance and patience. (Colossians 1:9–11)

But he said to me, "My grace is sufficient for you, for my power is made perfect in weakness." Therefore I will boast all the more gladly about my weaknesses, so that Christ's power may rest on me. That is why, for Christ's sake, I delight in weaknesses, in insults, in hardships, in persecutions, in difficulties. For when I am weak, then I am strong. (2 Corinthians 12:9–10)

Consider it pure joy, my brothers and sisters, whenever you face trials of many kinds, because you know that the testing of your faith produces perseverance. Let perseverance finish its work so that you may be mature and complete, not lacking anything. (James 1:2–4)

I love that we get to see in these verses that the suffering will end. He will restore us. There's a reason for this. He will strengthen us. He will make us strong in the midst of our feeling weak. And there's a perfecting of us that's happening in the process.

When we think the process of longsuffering is unbearable, we must remember it would be deadly for God to put us up on that solid rock before we are strong, firm, and steadfast. And it would be cruel for Him to require us to sing before we have a song.

There is purpose to this process. Yes, the process will be so messy, so full of slime and mud and mire and cries for help that you can't help but wonder whether they are being heard or not.

They are. As I said before, God isn't far off. He's just far more interested in your being prepared than in your being comfortable. God will take every cry you've uttered and arrange those sounds into a glorious song. He will add it to His symphony of compassion.

You will have a starring solo in which those notes birthed from tears will help ease the ache of another. Those around you will see you standing on a solid rock and hear the glorious echoes of good things bellowing from your belly. The enemy will shake and quake and shrink back afraid. He's terrified of that girl. He's terrified of *you*.

You are anchored to the hope of God that so few ever truly find. You, dear longsuffering soul, are a Job of your time. One who will be misjudged and misunderstood. The enemy will try to trip you and rip you to shreds with the hurtful hisses that all this longsuffering is for nothing. Don't you dare listen.

I'm holding a purple heart in my hand that tells me something different. And it's not just for me. It's for you too. I knew it the minute the counselor put it in my hand, it should be pinned on your chest too. And if you were here with me in my quiet house today, I'd do just that.

Close your eyes and breathe. You're brave and beautiful and handpicked. A decorated soldier in this horrible battle with a glorious ending.

Oh, my longsuffering friend, hang on. Keep walking your tightrope, and I'll keep walking mine. Keep looking for His presence in your process, and I will too. Together we will make it all the way across. And if you make it through your longsuffering journey before I do, come cheer me on. Today, I'm still a girl in the middle. But I'm a girl who is one step farther than ever before, on my way to a really good promise!

My toes might still be cold when I go to bed tonight, but my longsuffering heart definitely won't be.

GOING *to the* WELL

To hope is to acknowledge reality in the very same breath that I acknowledge God's sovereignty.

REMEMBER:

- When things stay hard for a long time, every day feels more like walking on a tightrope than a solid and secure road into the future.
- My hope is tied to the unchanging promise of God.
- I know I must walk through God's process before I see His fulfilled promise.
- God isn't picking on me. God is picking me to personally live out one of His promises.
- I've got to walk through the low places of the process before I'm perfectly equipped to live the promise.
- Not only is His presence in the process, but there's also a purpose in the process.
- The process isn't a cruel way to keep you from the promise; it's the exact preparation you'll need to handle the promise.
- God is far more interested in your being prepared than in your being comfortable.

RECEIVE:

And the God of all grace, who called you to his eternal glory in Christ, after you have suffered a little while, will himself restore you and make you strong, firm, and steadfast. (1 Peter 5:10)

Also read:

Job 42
Psalm 40:1–4
2 Corinthians 12:9–10
Colossians 1:9–11
James 1:2–4

REFLECT:

- Think back on what we talked about regarding God's presence, process, purpose, preparation, and promise. How does this help you with your own disappointments?
- Consider the list of verses that speaks to the process. Which one resonates most deeply with you?
- What promises of God are you desperate to see fulfilled right now?

Father,

I confess there are days when it feels like You have forgotten me, maybe even abandoned me, because this battle has raged on for so long. And I confess there are times I get tired of hoping, weary from waiting, and I wonder just how much longer it will all go on. Thank You for reminding me that there is purpose to this process and that I'm not walking through any of this alone. You are my strength. You are my hope. You are my song. Help me fix my eyes once again on Your promises. And remind me to keep my hope tied to You and You alone.

In Jesus' name, amen.

WHEN G

GIVES Y

THAN YO

HANDLE

OD

U MORE

U CAN

Chapter 7

WHEN GOD GIVES YOU MORE
THAN YOU CAN HANDLE

*E*very syllable of the last chapter is true. I've felt pumped up and ready to keep going, embrace these hardships, be one of the rare souls who truly does persevere.

And then life.

All the stuff and then more stuff.

The ink hadn't even dried from the last chapter when the need for another mammogram turned into the need for a biopsy.

Everyone, including my doctor, assured me there was little reason for concern. I had no family history of breast cancer. My mom had gone through the call-back and biopsy journey herself, but everything had turned out fine in the end. I am young(ish) and healthy. Plus, I'd already had the unexpected medical crisis with my colon last year. Surely, that situation plus everything else I'd been going through was enough.

Everything was in my favor.

Except I knew when Art and I heard my doctor's serious tone, everything wasn't okay.

"Lysa, you have cancer. They will tell you more when you go for your appointment today, but I wanted to go ahead and let you know I read the pathology report. I'm so sorry."

I wish I could properly describe what happened in that moment. Everything around me got incredibly quiet and seemed to move very slowly. I could hear the doctor continuing to talk, but I couldn't make out his words. I could see Art tearing up. I could feel words trying to form in my mouth, but there was no energy to speak. I knew I should probably cry, but no tears seemed available. Maybe I'd used them all up?

I'd just finished the previous chapter, and I absolutely believed with all my heart that there's a promise and a process and the presence of God was in the midst of my life. But in that moment

He felt distant and mysterious. I felt stunned. And then I felt okay. And then I felt stunned again.

My feelings couldn't seem to land. I wanted to be peaceful. But then I didn't want to be peaceful. I wanted to hold it together. But then falling apart seemed quite reasonable.

I stayed quiet.

I reached out and squeezed Art's hand.

No need for any words when words wouldn't help right then. We drove to where the doctor told us to drive in near silence.

We walked in, and they ushered us to a room with tissue boxes and books written by cancer survivors. There was a stack of brochures about handling a cancer diagnosis. The lights were warm, the room was cold, and the chairs were pink.

I wondered if this could be some sort of awful mistake and at any minute the doctor would apologize and send us on our way.

I wondered about the woman who sat in this pink chair just before me. And the woman who'd sit in that same chair after me. Where would they go after they got the news? Do you just get in your car and go back to work? Or meet a friend for coffee? Or run home to your bed and pull the covers over your head?

Who do you call? And how do you tell them?

There's no easy way to attach the word *cancer* to your world and not make all who love you cry.

I kept thinking about that statement everyone loves to throw out in times like these: "God won't give you more than you can handle." But that's not actually in the Bible.

God does say He won't allow us to be tempted beyond what we can bear and that He always provides a way out (1 Corinthians 10:13). But that's not the same as God not giving us more than we can handle.

He sometimes will allow more and more and more.

I knew this. And now I was sitting in a pink chair living it.

And, as I type these words, I know I'm not the only one who feels they've been given more than they can handle. I see the wide-eyed expressions on people all the time. Grief upon grief. Hurt upon hurt. Heartbreak upon heartbreak. Addiction upon addiction. Diagnosis upon diagnosis. Disappointment upon disappointment. The world is filled with people who are dealt more than they can handle. And, surprisingly, the Bible is also filled with people who were given more than they could handle.

The apostle Paul wrote:

> For we do not want you to be uninformed, brothers and sisters, about the troubles we experienced in the province of Asia. We were under great pressure, far beyond our ability to endure, so that we despaired of life itself. Indeed, we felt we had received the sentence of death. But this happened that we might not rely on ourselves but on God, who raises the dead. (2 Corinthians 1:8–9)

God doesn't expect us to handle this. He wants us to hand this over to Him.

He doesn't want us to rally more of our own strength. He wants us to rely solely on His strength.

God doesn't expect us to handle this. He wants us to hand this over to Him.

If we keep walking around, thinking that God won't give us more than we can handle, we set ourselves up to be suspicious of God. We know we are facing things that are too much for us. We are bombarded with burdens. We are weighed down with wondering. And we are all trying to make sense of things that don't make sense. Before we can move forward in a healthy way, we must first acknowledge the truth about our insufficiency.

Cancer is more than I can handle . . .

. . . on my own.

I closed my eyes and silently asked God to come and sit in the empty pink chair near me, Art, and the doctor. I needed God to show me His perspective so I could set my perspective. But it didn't come right away. And that frustrated me. I was filled with fear and questions like, *Why this? Why now? Why me?*

I could feel my emotions starting to unravel and my resolve to trust God slipping. It was too much. I didn't want to keep trying so hard to trust God. I was tired of trying to make sense of this life that isn't supposed to be this way.

I went to bed that night seriously contemplating running away to Montana to hide from my life. I could be a waitress in a breakfast diner. I had been a waitress when I was in my early twenties and loved it. Life was simpler then. Serving up plates of bacon and eggs and toast sounded so appealing. But cancer would follow me. The hurt would follow me. And even my wrestling with whether or not I could trust God would certainly follow me whether I moved to Montana or just crawled in a hole somewhere.

The story I started telling myself was that life would never get any better. My mind became fixated on all that pointed to this season of suffering being my new normal.

I woke up with panicked feelings. I walked around with panicked feelings. I went to bed with panicked feelings.

I knew my thinking had to change.

I couldn't escape my realities. I had to face them. I had to walk through them. But maybe if I changed my thinking I could trust God in the midst of them.

Thinking about everything I didn't know wasn't getting me anywhere. So, I started listing things I did know.

And the main thing I know? I know God is good. I didn't know the details of God's good plan, but I could make His goodness the starting place to renew my perspective.

So now let me tell the story of all these recent events using God's goodness as the central theme. Had things not blown up between Art and me last summer, I never would have hit the pause button on life to go get a mammogram. I would have waited. But because I had a mammogram at that exact time, the doctors caught a cancer that needed to be caught. And because they caught a cancer that needed to be caught, I had every fighting chance to beat this cancer.

You see, we're all living out a story, but then there's the story we tell ourselves. We just need to make sure what we're telling ourselves is the right story. And the right story is, yes, God will give us more than we can handle. But He always has eventual good in mind.

We see more and more unnecessary heartbreak. But God sees the exact pieces and parts that must be added right now to protect us, provide for us, and prepare us with more and more of His strength working through us. We don't have to like it, but maybe knowing this can help us live through it.

I learned about these very necessary "pieces and parts" one day when a couple of girls introduced themselves while standing in line to get some take-out food at a restaurant near my house. Pauline and Jessica had both read my book *Uninvited*. We chatted for a minute about what God had been teaching them, and then the topic of what I'd be writing next came up. I told them about this book and the revelation God had given me about dust. Jessica's eyes lit up. Her mom is a professional potter.

As I shared how, when we place our dust into God's hands and

He mixes it with His living water, the clay that's formed can then be made into anything, she smiled so big. She'd seen clay being formed into many beautiful things when placed into her mother's hands. And then she shared something with me that made my jaw drop.

She told me that wise potters not only know how to form beautiful things from clay, but they also know how important it is to add some of the dust from previously broken pieces of pottery to the new clay. This type of dust is called "grog." To get this grog, the broken pieces must be shattered to dust just right. If the dust is shattered too finely, then it won't add any structure to the new clay. And if it's not shattered enough, the grog will be too coarse and make the potter's hands bleed.

But when shattered just right, the grog dust added to the new clay will enable the potter to form the clay into a larger and stronger vessel than ever before. And it can go through fires much hotter as well. Plus, when glazed, these pieces end up having a much more beautiful, artistic look to them than they would have otherwise.[4]

Jessica smiled and said, "C'mon, that will preach, right?!"

Oh, it absolutely did. I kept thinking about what Jessica shared and how it might relate to my season of suffering. What if the clay made from all the other dust currently in my life could be strengthened by this newly added broken piece?

And then I read Isaiah 45:9: "Woe to those who quarrel with their Maker, those who are nothing but potsherds among the potsherds on the ground. Does the clay say to the potter, 'What are you making?' Does your work say, 'The potter has no hands'?"

God is making something beautiful out of my life. I know that. So, why question what He sees as the necessary ingredients to make my life stronger and more beautiful than ever? Sure, my diagnosis added some more brokenness, but even this could be used for my good.

I kept reading that verse from Isaiah and decided to do a little investigation into the term *potsherd*.

A potsherd is a broken piece of pottery.

Interestingly enough, a potsherd was also mentioned in the story of Job when he was inflicted with an awful disease.

> So Satan went out from the presence of the LORD and afflicted Job with painful sores from the soles of his feet to the crown of his head. Then Job took a piece of broken pottery and scraped himself with it as he sat among the ashes.
>
> His wife said to him, "Are you still maintaining your integrity? Curse God and die!"
>
> He replied, "You are talking like a foolish woman. Shall we accept good from God, and not trouble?"
>
> In all this, Job did not sin in what he said. (Job 2:7–10)

A broken potsherd can lie on the ground and be nothing more than a constant reminder of brokenness. It can also be used to continue to scrape us and hurt us even more when kept in our hands.

Or, when placed in our Master's hands, the Master Potter can be entrusted to take that potsherd, shatter it just right, and then use it in the remolding of me to make me stronger and even more beautiful.

When I understood this, I saw that in all my circumstances God was keeping me moldable while adding even more strength and beauty in the process.

I don't want to have cancer.

There's no part of my human brain that thinks cancer is fair for any precious person who receives this diagnosis. God didn't cause this potsherd reality in my life. It's the result of living in this broken world between two gardens.

Since I do have cancer, however, I don't want this broken reality to just be a potsherd wasted on the ground or something I keep in my hand that hurts me more. I must take even this and entrust it to the Lord.

Take this, Lord, and shatter it just right, so I can be made stronger, more beautiful, and able to withstand fires as never before. I believe that You see things I cannot see. And You have eventual good in mind.

This perspective didn't take away my cancer. But it did take away the feeling I had to figure this out on my own. It took the weight of it all out of my hands and helped me release it to God.

When we hit the place in our lives where we finally realize some things are truly more than we can handle, we will throw our hands up in surrender. And that surrender can happen in one of two ways.

We might surrender to the enemy, giving in to those feelings that this isn't fair, God isn't there, and God isn't good. Or, we can surrender to God. This kind of surrender isn't giving in; it's giving up! Giving up carrying the weight of all that's too much for us to our God, who not only can carry it but use it for good. When we know the truth about the amazing things God can do with the dust and the potsherds of life, we won't surrender to the negative lies of the enemy. Instead, we will lift our hands to the Potter.

So, now that we know we need to surrender the weight of these broken pieces of our lives to God, how exactly do we do that?

God is who He says He is, and He will do what He says He will do. But to partner with Him in His work of transformation in our lives, we must seek Him with all our hearts. It's our choice whether we stay stuck in our hurt or get renewed in our hearts.

There are some frequently quoted verses that teach us this. But before I quote the verses, I want to give us some context. In

It's our choice

whether we stay

stuck in our hurt or

get renewed in our

the book of Jeremiah, we find that the children of Israel were going to be carried into captivity by Babylon for seventy years. Think about how long seventy years is. If we had to go to prison today for seventy years, for most of us that would mean we'd probably die in captivity. Seventy years feels impossibly long, incredibly unfair, and horribly hard. It would seem like a lifetime hardship without a lifeline of hope. Talk about longsuffering. Talk about feeling as if no good thing could ever come from this. Talk about needing God's perspective like never before! But here's what God told the people of Israel: "When seventy years are completed for Babylon, I will come to you and fulfill my good promise to bring you back to this place" (Jeremiah 29:10).

This is the scene and the setting where we then get these glorious promises that I love to cling to:

> For I know the plans I have for you . . . plans to prosper you and
> not to harm you, plans to give you hope and a future. Then you
> will call on me and come and pray to me, and I will listen to
> you. You will seek me and find me when you seek me with all
> your heart. I will be found by you. (Jeremiah 29:11–14)

When we seek God, we see God. We don't see His physical form, but we see Him at work and can start to see more of what He sees. Trust grows. If our hearts are willing to trust Him, He will entrust to us more and more of His perspective. Matthew 5:8 teaches us, "blessed are the pure in heart, for they will see God." If we want to see Him in our circumstances and see His perspective, we must seek Him, His ways, and His Word. That's where we find His good plans and promises for hope and a future.

If we find ourselves in an incredibly disappointing place—a place we don't want to be—a very long season of suffering that just goes on and on, or one we know will not be changed on this side of eternity, it's easy to start feeling that some of God's good plans don't apply to us.

It's easy to slip into the mentality that we somehow fell through the cracks of God's good plans. Things are too final. The ink is too dry. The page has been turned. Their heart is too hard. Your heart is too hurt. The doctors have said impossible. The account is too bankrupt. The biological clock has run out. One hard thing just gives way to another hard thing, and then more hard things. And there's just been one too many days full of unanswered prayers.

But the truth is, God is closer than we often realize. He sees things we don't see, and He knows things we don't know. He has a perspective from where He sits that allows Him to see all things—the past, the present, and the future—from the day we are conceived to the day we return to dust and even beyond that into eternity.

> Listen to me . . . you whom I have upheld since your birth, and have carried since you were born. Even to your old age and grey hairs I am he, I am he who will sustain you. I have made you and I will carry you. I will sustain you and I will rescue you . . . I am God, and there is no other; I am God, and there is none like me. I make known the end from the beginning, from ancient times, what is still to come. I say, "My purpose will stand, and I will do all that I please." From the east I summon a bird of prey; from a far-off land, a man to fulfill my purpose. What I have said, that I will bring about; what I have planned, that I will do. (Isaiah 46:3–4, 9–11)

This was true for the Israelites. And it's true for us.

For them, the news that they would be in captivity for seventy years was absolute reality. But the truth that God had a good plan and a purpose not to harm them but to give them a future and a hope—that promise was very much in process all the while they were in captivity.

This is how we, too, can surrender the weight of our long-suffering journeys to God: by having a higher perspective in our present realities. The seemingly impossible work of redemption is always possible with God. In other words, we need to remember the difference between news and truth.

News comes at us to tell us what we are dealing with.

Truth comes from God and then helps us process all we are dealing with.

News and truth aren't always one and the same.

My sweet friend Shaunti Feldhahn reminded me of this a few years ago. An e-mail she sent me about a difficulty I was walking through said, "Lysa, this is news. This is not truth."

What the doctor gave me was news. Honest news based on test results and medical facts.

But what I have access to is a truth that transcends news. The restoration that is impossible with man's limitations is always possible for a limitless God. Truth is what factors God into the equation.

I find myself looking at the word *impossible* a little differently today.

News and truth aren't always one and the same.

Impossible, when looked at in light of Shaunti's note, could be completely different if I just stuck a little apostrophe between the first two letters. Then it becomes *I'm-Possible*. God is the great I AM. Therefore, He is my possibility for hope and healing.

I'm-Possible is a much more comforting way to look at anything that feels quite impossible—anything that feels like it's too much for me to handle. Instead of saying God won't give me more than I can handle, maybe I can just simply say, "God's got a handle on all I'm facing."

I suspect many of us have things in our lives that feel impossible. Maybe you just got some bad news. News of an impossible financial situation. News of an impossible job situation. News of an impossible kid situation. News of an impossible friend situation. News of an impossible medical situation.

Whatever news you just got or will get, I pray Shaunti's advice helps you too.

That is news.

And *this* is God's Truth:

I AM THE WAY AND THE TRUTH AND THE LIFE.

"I am the way and the truth and the life. No one comes to the Father except through me." (John 14:6)

I AM FOREVER FAITHFUL.

He is the Maker of heaven and earth,
    the sea, and everything in them—
He remains faithful forever.

(Psalm 146:6)

I AM WITH YOU.

So do not fear, for I am with you;
    do not be dismayed, for I am your God.

I will strengthen you and help you;
  I will uphold you with my righteous right hand.

(Isaiah 41:10)

I AM HOLDING YOU.

Yet I am always with you;
  you hold me by my right hand.

(Psalm 73:23)

I AM YOUR HIDING PLACE.

You are my hiding place;
  you will protect me from trouble
  and surround me with songs of deliverance.

(Psalm 32:7)

One of the greatest comforts to me through all this has been knowing that somehow God will use it for good. And that God will be my possible in the midst of what can sometimes feel so impossible.

Of course, I still have those less spiritually secure moments when the broken pieces seem to be piling up too high and I feel like I'm going to lose my mind. And cry. And pitch a little hissy fit.

But how thankful I am for the Great I AM. The One who will absolutely guide me in truth and teach me, the One I put my hope in all day long (Psalm 25:5). Yes, He can handle all the things I know I can't, and I trust Him to take my broken and make it beautiful.

GOING *to the* WELL

God doesn't expect us to handle this. He wants us to hand this over to Him.

REMEMBER:

- God doesn't want us to rally more of our own strength. He wants us to rely solely on His strength.
- If we keep walking around thinking that God won't give us more than we can handle, we set ourselves up to be suspicious of God.
- God is making something beautiful out of my life.
- Surrendering to God isn't giving in—it's giving up! Giving up carrying the weight of all that's too much for us to our God.
- It's our choice whether we stay stuck in our hurt or get renewed in our hearts.
- God isn't far off and distant: He's closer than we often realize.
- Is this news or truth?
- The restoration that is impossible with man's limitations is always possible for a limitless God.

RECEIVE:

We do not want you to be uninformed, brothers and sisters, about the troubles we experienced in the province of Asia. We were under great pressure, far beyond our ability to endure, so that we despaired of life itself. Indeed, we felt we had received the sentence of death. But this happened that we might not rely on ourselves but on God, who raises the dead. (2 Corinthians 1:8–9)

Also read:
Job 2:7–10
Psalm 25:5
Isaiah 45:9; 46:3–4, 9–11
Jeremiah 29:10–14
Matthew 5:8
1 Corinthians 10:13
Truth verses: Psalm 32:7; 73:23; 146:6; Isaiah 41:10; John 14:6

REFLECT:

- In what ways are you questioning how God is making your life stronger and more beautiful than ever?
- What broken pieces do you need to surrender to God?

Father,

I come to You today, a woman worn out from trying to do everything in my own strength. A woman ready to accept Your invitation to surrender. Today I say that I give up. I give up carrying the weight of all that's too much for me. Take this, Lord. Take all of this hard and all of this hurt and shatter it just right, so I can be made stronger, more beautiful, and able to withstand fires like never before. I trust Your love for me. I trust Your plans for me. And I trust You will use all of this for good.

In Jesus' name, amen.

LETTING
WHAT'S
ME BAC

GO OF
OLDING
K

Chapter 8

LETTING GO OF WHAT'S HOLDING ME BACK

*H*ere's what I fear at this point of our journey together. I fear you having a picture of my messy that's way too tidy. That maybe you've looked straight on at my faith and made some fine-sounding assumptions and conclusions that are impressive but not true. If you do this, you may think when things get messy in the process and progress of your journey, that maybe your faith isn't strong enough.

Dear one . . . that's not true.

Weak moments don't make weak faith. Weak moments make us even more aware of our need to press in to faith. A faith in God that helps us know that what we see isn't all there is. Weak moments are also clues telling us what needs to be addressed right now in this part of the journey. Don't beat yourself up for weak moments. But don't ignore them either.

I've learned to pay attention to my weak moments, the moments where my hurt gets triggered and I have an out-of-proportion reaction to a situation. When my instant reaction is to cry or yell or kick into control mode or freak out in whatever way I feel is so very justifiable, I know there's more to this story than passing hormones. There are unattended wounds.

Today it was a question that someone asked that should have been a simple dialogue. However, because there was still past hurt tied to the subject matter, this question sparked some feelings that led to some thoughts that led to an all-out flood of unresolved pain. My face went stoic, but inside my brain, my emotions came out swinging wild and unrestrained, stewing with hurt and spewing sharp words. Suddenly there were piles of files that opened up in my brain categorizing mounting evidence of why my feelings were justified and my thoughts true. I started recalling other times this person made me feel this way. I had these other past conversations with this person logged away in folders inside my mind labeled "proof to be used as needed."

And oh what a little collection I had. Proof they didn't have my best interest in mind. Proof they couldn't be trusted.

In reality, I knew this was a person who loved me. I had forgiven them for the things in this file, so why did I suddenly remember all their worst with keen precision and great detail? They had plenty of wonderful deposits in my life from recent months that I could point to to make the case that they were safe. However, because their question felt scary, everything about them suddenly felt scary. Every issue from our past compounded this present situation.

I was having a hard time finding a reasonable rhythm for my breath. I wanted this person away from me. At the same time I wanted them to come close and declare their question idiotic and take it back. I wanted them to read my mind and tell me I was right to feel this way and then suddenly present me a legally binding document by which they could swear they'd never ever hurt me again. Give me a guarantee for safety or give me the death of our relationship!

As I type these words, I can look back on the situation and see how much I was blowing everything out of proportion. But in the heat of the moment these feelings felt like the most logical thoughts I'd ever had. My most irrational thoughts gathered up all the hurt from what was in these files and held it up to the spark of hurt from the unexpected question I was being asked. And soon a roaring fire burst into existence. Unresolved past hurts make for fantastic kindling of the most tragic kind.

I had forgiven this person for the facts of what they'd done. I had said the words. But I had refused to let go of the labels I put on this person.

Uncaring.

Irresponsible.

Coldhearted.

Sometimes these labels protect us from toxic people. But sometimes they prevent us from truly forgiving and moving forward with even our healthy relationships. There's wisdom in knowing the difference.

I felt a deep-down knowing this was a safe person who didn't deserve the labels I'd placed on them. They had simply asked a question that should have taken one healthy conversation to resolve. But because past feelings fed my present hurt, I wasted hours of emotional energy mulling over this. My morning was derailed. My emotions were hijacked. And not one time in the whole deal did I remember I could make a better choice. Stellar, huh?

Maybe you, too, have these derailing moments in the midst of all the progress you've made. This isn't an indication that your healing isn't working. It's just an indication that you're a human still holding on to some hurt that needs to be resolved. And I am too.

This isn't a reason to condemn ourselves. But it is a call to action.

I've got some perspectives hindering me. I've got some unresolved hurts holding me back. There are still files in my mind that need to be cleaned out and cleared away. Otherwise, my efforts to move forward will have cords of attachment to my past hurt that are always threatening to pull me back and take me down.

But here's the gift of my very messy moments like these. They make me aware that there are some things to address. It's when I stop pretending I'm fine when I'm really not fine. It's when I stop to face what's really holding me back from moving forward. And not just limp forward or crawl forward burdened down from what I've been through but to run forward with great freedom. Hebrews 12:1–2 reminds us:

Therefore, since we are surrounded by such a great cloud of witnesses, let us throw off everything that hinders and the sin that so easily entangles. And let us run with perseverance the race marked out for us, fixing our eyes on Jesus, the pioneer and perfecter of faith. For the joy set before him he endured the cross, scorning its shame, and sat down at the right hand of the throne of God.

To be able to run free, we must do three things:

- We are to throw off what hinders us.
- We are to stay free of the entanglements of sin.
- We are to persevere by keeping our eyes on Jesus, who is the author of our story of faith.

Throwing Off What Hinders Us

In the situation I described earlier, the question that I was asked tapped right into a deep fear in my heart . . . the fear that I caused the added hardships in my life. And because I was carrying that fear, it didn't take much for my friend's question that leaned in that direction to be misunderstood. She was simply inquiring about a change I might need to make. But I heard her declaring this whole thing could have been prevented. That's not at all what she was implying, but it sure is what I had already been wrestling with deep in my heart. So it didn't take much for her question to tap into my fear.

It's not that I don't have some things to own. But, in this instance, I was holding myself accountable for things I didn't do. I was beating myself up for choices that were not my own. And the burden of this fear, this lie, was hindering me from moving forward in a healthier way, from hearing my friend's words without assigning hidden meanings to them.

I finally recognized if I could deal with this fear and learn how to have a more truth-filled perspective on circumstances I didn't choose or cause, I could probably more easily forgive future offenses that tapped into that fear. And I could have better reactions to questions and statements made by others. And maybe I could even get brave enough to get rid of the files of proof.

Maybe you have had your own version of this that made you feel like you were going to lose your mind and all evidence that you love Jesus. I understand. And I want us to deal with this. We'll get to dealing with sin that causes hardships in just a bit. But please hear me, sometimes hardship happens not because of what you've done but because of something God is doing and will eventually make right.

We see this in both the Old and the New Testaments. We saw this in the life of Job that we've already discussed. His friends were determined to identify what Job did to cause his hardship. But God made it clear that Job's friends were misguided in their accusations.

Jesus also made this same point in one of His interactions. Do you remember what I shared earlier about Jesus spitting into the dust, making mud from His saliva, and healing the blind man's eyes?

That account is told in John 9. But there's more I want to show you from that teaching. There's more to the story that will really help us.

As he went along, he saw a man blind from birth. His disciples asked him, "Rabbi, who sinned, this man or his parents, that he was born blind?"

"Neither this man nor his parents sinned," said Jesus, "but this happened so that the works of God might be displayed in him. As long as it is day, we must do the works of him who sent me. Night is coming, when no one can work. While I am in the world, I am the light of the world."

After saying this, he spit on the ground, made some mud with the saliva, and put it on the man's eyes. "Go," he told him, "wash in the Pool of Siloam" (This word means "Sent"). So the man went and washed and came home seeing. (John 9:1–7)

This man's blindness—his own form of hardship and longsuffering—wasn't because of choices he made or ones his parents made. This suffering was placed on him. But it was for a reason. He was handpicked to display the works of God. Through his story Jesus would shine the light of truth and hope for others' lives to not be so dark. And then Jesus brought healing out of the man's brokenness.

Just imagine, out of all the world, this man was chosen to proclaim truth and display the works of God! Yes, the man suffered blindness for a long time. But in hindsight we can see all the blessings in disguise that underlay his brokenness:

- He was the one who got touched personally by Jesus and experienced firsthand dust being turned into healing mud.
- He got to hear Jesus proclaim one of the seven "I am" statements as recorded in the book of John. Right before his healing he heard Jesus say, "I am the light of the world."
- He was offered a personal salvation invitation by Jesus Himself. Can you imagine how cool that will be for him when we all chat in heaven about how we came to know the Lord? He will be one of the few who gets to say his salvation

invitation came from a personal conversation with Jesus. (John 9:35–38)

- His story is recorded in the Bible, and we are still talking about him today!

While his story and his blessings are unique to him, rest assured when you are chosen for suffering, you are chosen for the blessing of displaying the works of God as well. What if the worst parts of your life are actually gateways to the very best parts you'd never want to do without?

Okay. I very much realize some of you want to throw this book across the room right now. Because being chosen for suffering feels like God is causing bad things to happen to you. It's a lot of pain with no up-front reward. But remember, God isn't causing this; He's allowing it. God isn't picking on us. He's handpicked us to be a display of His good works here on earth. And trust me, in eternity you will want to be chosen for this. (I'll explain this later in the book, but for now, know that your reward is coming!)

If only we could see the full picture that God sees. If only we could see all the good God will surely do through us and for us. If we could even catch a glimpse of God's perspective, I don't think we would want to throw the book. Hang our heads. Shake our fists. Stomp our feet. Or continue logging all of those past hurts. I think we would simply say, "Okay, God chose me for this. And I can trust Him to lead me to it, through it, and past it. What feels horrible this day will be so very honorable that day."

What if the worst parts of your life are actually gateways to the very best parts you'd never want to do without?

Hang on to God's perspective. Give Jesus the weight of what

you're carrying. Stay unburdened and moldable. And you'll be a light to many others!

But, to keep us on track with Hebrews 12:1–2, we do need to also tackle our sin.

Getting Rid of Sin That So Easily Entangles

Hebrews 12:1–2 not only tells us not to carry the weight of those things placed on us but also to be very careful not to be held back by sin we bring on ourselves. Sin entangles and strangles our ability to run this race of life well. And I don't want to leave this chapter before we address the hardships in our lives caused by our sin.

Hear me, please. My cancer wasn't caused by any sin I committed. Many of the hardships people face—natural disasters, diseases, and unexplained losses—are the result of the fall we read about in Genesis 3. We may not be able to rid ourselves of these circumstances, but carrying the burden without God's hopeful perspective must be released. God often uses these heartbreaking instances as opportunities for us to be awakened to His restoration power in this life between two gardens. And to keep our hearts longing for the perfection of the final Eden where there will be no more hardships.

So that covers the hardships that happen to us. But other hardships I've faced in my life—other areas of longsuffering—were a direct result of my making choices outside of God's protective truth.

Both the problems placed on us and the problems within us due to sin need to be released—surrendered to God.

We talked about Job earlier. His hardship was not caused by

sin, and neither was the blind man's. But another man in the Bible brought on his burdens because of his sinful choices. His name was David.

After David was confronted about an adulterous affair he had with a woman named Bathsheba, he was horrified by just how far away from God his sin had taken him. There were consequences for his sin that could never be undone. Bathsheba's husband Uriah was killed. And the baby Bathsheba conceived with David during the affair died. These were realities in which the longsuffering effects would never go away. This "man after God's own heart" was utterly disappointed in himself, and the pain seemed to have no good purpose at all. But his story didn't end in the dust of despair! God was still working. God still had a plan. God was still molding and shaping David for a wonderful purpose—not just for him but to help others! David wrote Psalm 51 in response to his sin. And I think it's one of the best examples of getting rid of the "sin that so easily entangles us."

Watch the progression in his words.

The confession:

Have mercy on me, O God,
according to your unfailing love;
according to your great compassion
blot out my transgressions.
Wash away all my iniquity
and cleanse me from my sin.

For I know my transgressions
and my sin is always before me.
Against you, you only, have I sinned
and done what is evil in your sight;

so you are right in your verdict
and justified when you judge.
Surely I was sinful at birth,
sinful from the time my mother conceived me.
Yet you desired faithfulness even in the womb;
you taught me wisdom in that secret place.

(vv. 1–6)

The cleansing:

Cleanse me with hyssop, and I will be clean;
wash me, and I will be whiter than snow.
Let me hear joy and gladness;
let the bones you have crushed rejoice.
Hide your face from my sins
and blot out all my iniquity.

(vv. 7–9)

The creating:

Create in me a pure heart, O God,
and renew a steadfast spirit within me.
Do not cast me from your presence
or take your Holy Spirit from me.
Restore to me the joy of your salvation
and grant me a willing spirit, to sustain me.

(vv. 10–12)

The calling:

Then I will teach transgressors your ways,
so that sinners will turn back to you.
Deliver me from the guilt of bloodshed, O God,

> you who are God my Savior,
>
> > and my tongue will sing of your righteousness.
>
> Open my lips, Lord,
>
> > and my mouth will declare your praise.
>
> > > > (vv. 13–15)

Isn't that amazing? Do you see the progression of how God took the dust of David's sin and remolded him? David **confessed**. He asked God to **cleanse** him. He asked God to **create** within him a new heart. And then a **calling** was formed.

David's deepest desperation led to a great revelation from God.

And the same can be true for us when we surrender to the Lord.

David's temptation and deception by the evil one turned into a testimony and declaration about the goodness of our God.

And the same is true for us when we surrender to the Lord.

David's season of confession, cleansing, and having a new heart created within him couldn't be skipped or rushed. Every step was necessary for this to eventually become a season of restoration and the fulfilling of his calling.

And, again, the same is true for us when we surrender to the Lord.

Notice that David wrote in verse 13 above, "Then I will" not "Now I will."

Sin breaks trust. Therefore, we can't expect God to entrust a calling to us before our full confession, cleansing, and having a new heart created in place of our broken heart. When trust has been shattered, it has to be rebuilt with believable behavior in our actions and reactions over time.

So, in time, David healed and rebuilt trust. Then he could teach others what he learned so others tempted with this same sin would turn back to God. When we go through a season like

My deepest

desperation can

lead to a great

revelation from

God.

this, we can focus on learning about the compassionate nature of God and how to extend that compassion to others. In turn, it will be part of our calling. Just as David's pain turned into purpose, this can be true for us and the things we've done as well. Our longsuffering won't seem nearly as long or nearly as painful when we know God's perspective is to use it all for good.

Persevering by Keeping Our Eyes on Jesus

Here's how Eugene Peterson paraphrased Hebrews 12:1–3:

> Do you see what this means—all these pioneers who blazed the way, all these veterans cheering us on? It means we'd better get on with it. Strip down, start running—and never quit! No extra spiritual fat, no parasitic sins. Keep your eyes on Jesus, who both began and finished this race we're in. Study how he did it. Because he never lost sight of where he was headed—that exhilarating finish in and with God—he could put up with anything along the way: Cross, shame, whatever. And now he's there, in the place of honor, right alongside God. When you find yourselves flagging in your faith, go over that story again, item by item, that long litany of hostility he plowed through. That will shoot adrenaline into your souls!
> (THE MESSAGE)

I love that Eugene gives us the secret of being a person who keeps going. Let's call it the secret of being steadfast. Jesus lived it so we could know it. Let's look again at one specific part of the passage: "Because [Jesus] never lost sight of where he was headed . . . he could put up with anything along the way." That's why we must keep our eyes on Him and go over His story—the Bible—again and again.

This is how we get through this life between two gardens. This is how we make sense of things that don't make sense. This is how we can believe God is good when life isn't good. This is how we can face hurt upon hurt, disappointment upon disappointment, longsuffering upon longsuffering, and still run our race with oxygen filling our lungs, peace filling our minds, and joy filling our hearts.

This is how we can accept reality but live reassured. This is how we wrestle well between our faith and our feelings.

Don't lose sight of where we are headed. Let's keep our eyes on Jesus, who will show us how to put up with anything along the way.

Last year, God showed me a picture of how He wants me to be as I do life from here. I'm not really a "see some sort of vision" kind of girl. So at first I thought it was just my imagination wandering off for a minute. But then I felt an impression on my heart that this wasn't random; this really was from God.

What I saw inside my mind was a beautiful flower made from paper-thin glass. I looked at it from all sides and admired the way it was formed. Then I saw a hand reaching out and wrapping itself around the glass flower. But as the hand closed around it, the glass popped and shattered. The glass was delicately beautiful but too fragile to be worked with.

Then I saw the same flower formed out of shiny metal. And the hand reached out and wrapped itself around the flower and held it for a few seconds. But then once again the hand closed around it. Only this time nothing happened to the flower. It didn't change in any way. And I could tell the harder the hand pressed, the more pain the steel flower was causing the hand. The steel was strong but not moldable. The metal flower was too hard to give way to the hand's desired working.

Then I saw the same flower made from a white clay. Every detail was the same except now when the hand reached out and closed around it, the flower moved with the hand. The clay squeezed out between the hand's fingers. The hand folded and twisted and worked with the clay until suddenly an even more beautiful flower emerged.

The clay was delicately beautiful but not too fragile. The clay was strong enough to hold its shape but soft enough to allow the hand to reshape it as needed. And in the end, the clay flower wound up being the most beautifully shaped of them all.

And that's when I finally felt I could understand a bit of God's perspective. God loves the parts of me that are delicately beautiful but He doesn't want me to be fragile like that glass. God made me to be strong but He doesn't want me to get hard and unable to be molded like metal.

He wants me like the clay, able to stand firm but still able to be molded and reformed into whatever purpose He has for me. And the only way I can do this is by keeping my eyes on Jesus. Always.

I knew I'd be able to process life better if this was my perspective too.

Just a few months after God gave me the vision of the flower, I was teaching the dust message at a conference with LifeWay called "The Word Alive." One of the things that makes this conference so different is that the women attending are provided with elements by which they can experience God working through the teachings in very personal ways. Because I was teaching about dust being mixed with God's living water to make clay and how beautiful and new things can be made from clay, each attendee received a small lump of clay.

I watched the women form their clay into their own creations of beauty. It was a profound time, seeing them think about the shattered "dust" places of their lives and touch and mold the clay just like God wants to do with them. There were so many meaningful shapes, but there was one that especially made me smile. It was an amazing flower. Very similar to the one in my vision months earlier.

God was comforting this woman with the same comfort He'd given me. My heart was filled with joy. I felt a sense of redemption. And a renewed purpose rose up in me. My circumstances hadn't changed, but my certainty in God's plan being good had. I could see with my own eyes that none of my tears would be wasted. It wasn't the full picture—it didn't give me all the answers—but it was just enough to help me keep going.

And it wasn't because I was standing on a stage in front of a crowd. It was because I saw one woman's flower. I saw one woman being helped by my story. I saw one person's tears ease and hope rise. Yes, because I had dared to break my own secrecy, she could break hers. What a gift.

My story intersected with her story. God arranged all of eternity to make sure that I'd be right there at that moment and so would she. He was carrying each of us separately, but on that day He carried us together. My life touched hers and made her feel less alone, less broken, less hopeless. Her life touched mine and reminded me I had lessons I could share from my brokenness that were valuable and helpful.

I made a difference, and what a difference that made in me. Wallowing in my suffering produces nothing but red eyes, bedhead, and a heart full of despair. But walking out the good things God purposes from my suffering produces eyes of hope, clearheaded thoughts, and a heart full of real joy.

Whether our hardships and disappointments are because of things we've done, like David, or things placed on us, like the blind man, God's perspective is that it will all be for good. He will allow us to suffer sometimes, but He won't let that suffering be wasted. And He will use that suffering to shape us, mold us, and make us even better prepared for our purpose if we throw off what hinders us, stay free of the entanglements of sin, and persevere by keeping our eyes on Jesus.

When we are afflicted, we are being made more effective!

When we are afflicted, we are being made more effective! That's how we can "glory in our sufferings":

Therefore, since we have been justified through faith, we have peace with God through our Lord Jesus Christ, through whom we have gained access by faith into this grace in which we now stand. And we boast in the hope of the glory of God. Not only so, but we also glory in our sufferings, because we know that suffering produces perseverance; perseverance, character; and character, hope. (Romans 5:1–4)

Isn't it a beautiful thing that keeping our eyes on the Lord makes our burden light? And then He takes our burden and uses it as light? In the end, not only will our suffering produce perseverance—endurance for our race—but it will bring forth hope. Glorious, glorious hope for all.

GOING *to the* WELL

What if the worst parts of your life are actually gateways to the very best parts you'd never want to do without?

REMEMBER:

- Sometimes hardship happens not because of what you've done but because of something God is doing.
- When you are chosen for suffering, you are chosen for the blessing of displaying the works of God.
- God isn't causing this pain and suffering—He's allowing it.
- Sin entangles and strangles our ability to run this race of life well.
- My deepest desperation can lead to a great revelation from God.
- God will use suffering to shape us, mold us, and make us even better prepared for our purpose.
- When we are afflicted, we are being made more effective!
- In the end, not only will our suffering produce perseverance—endurance for our race—but it will bring forth hope.

RECEIVE:

Therefore, since we are surrounded by such a great cloud of witnesses, let us throw off everything that hinders and the sin that so easily entangles. And let us run with perseverance the race marked out for us, fixing our eyes on Jesus, the pioneer and perfecter of faith. For the joy set before him he endured the cross, scorning its shame, and sat down at the right hand of the throne of God. (Hebrews 12:1–2)

Also read:
Psalm 51:1–15
John 9:1–7, 35–38
Romans 5:1–4

REFLECT:

- What heavy weights are hindering you and need to be thrown off? (Hebrews 12:1)
- What sins are easily entangling you? (Hebrews 12:1)
- What would it look like for you to persevere right now? (Hebrews 12:2)
- What joy has been set before you and will help you endure? (Hebrews 12:2)

Father,

This is what I want: to run with perseverance the race You have set before me. To keep moving forward even when the enemy's taunts are deafening and my own flesh is demanding that I give up and turn back. Open my eyes to see anything and everything that is hindering me. Search my heart. Examine my life. And help me grab firmly onto the truth that You are for me and not against me. You are not a God who picks on me. You are a God who has handpicked me. And I want to live a life that brings You glory. Help me catch my breath today, Lord. I'm ready to get moving once again.

In Jesus' name, amen.

EXPO

THE E

SING

NEMY

EXPOSING THE ENEMY

*D*o you remember what I wrote about the enemy in the first chapter of this book? If he can isolate us, he can influence us. And his favorite of all entry points is through our disappointments.

Knowing this, I feel such an urgency to help us better understand how he operates and how we can live free from the entanglements of darkness. I want to unpack this for us. But as I do, I want you to remember the symphony of compassion in God's words. And the tenderness by which all these words are written. There is no condemnation here. But there is help and hope. I don't want any of us to stay isolated and intimidated and influenced by the enemy.

This isn't to expose you or me. This is to expose the enemy.

Also, please don't let any of this talk of our enemy stir up fear in you. This information about our enemy isn't meant to scare us but to inform us. And, ultimately, protect us and free us.

I'm preaching this message to myself. But as you listen in, I bet you'll find the reason God made sure you were reading these words on this day.

The enemy uses disappointments to cause so much trouble in an unsettled heart. A heart hungry for something to ease the ache of disappointment is especially susceptible to the most dangerous forms of desire. Especially when that heart isn't being proactive about taking in truth and staying in community with healthy, humble people living out that truth.

Remember, dangerous desires birthed inside our unsettled disappointments are nothing but a setup for a takedown. A quick rise to a hard fall.

A dear friend of mine has lived this. And wants you and me to see what she didn't see until serious destruction and devastation happened.

This friend moved out of town five years ago, and though we

Dangerous *desires* birthed inside our unsettled disappointments are nothing but a setup for a takedown.

had the best of intentions to stay connected, life happened. We kept up through occasional phone calls and text exchanges, but it was hard. We drifted. I missed her, but the long distance made staying close harder than we had expected.

So I was thrilled when she texted me and said she was coming to one of my speaking events a couple of hours from where she now lived.

The week before we were going to see each other, I bought a cute new outfit and didn't eat any bread. Because, hey girl, you are so worth the effort!

I was in a playful mood when we first sat down at our re-connection lunch. And while she smiled and played along, I sensed that something was off. Really off.

I could feel it. I could almost smell the smoke of destruction. And where there's smoke, there's always a fire. So, I refused to brush it off. I couldn't brush it off. Alarm bells were going off in my mind and making my hands sweat. I looked deep into her eyes, and I simply said, "I know you aren't okay. Let me in."

She shut her eyes and inhaled sharply. Then there was a long breathy exhale that made her lips fall into a frown and her shoulders slump.

"I've done something awful. So awful I feel as if I'm going to die. Honestly, some days, I want to die."

My heart started drumming against the bones of my chest. Suddenly it felt as if the air was being sucked out of the room. I made myself mentally recite, "Don't panic. Don't panic. Don't panic," as I reached for her hand.

A story of compromise, deception, and marital betrayal spilled from her lips while tears spilled from her eyes.

It's heartbreaking to look into someone's eyes you deeply love and see sheer terror. She had made choices that slammed into her life like a wrecking ball. Her life no longer had soft edges and gentle places to land. Her choices had demolished what once was good into the sharp reality of a nightmare.

I knew the enemy was doing what he does best: stealing, killing, destroying (John 10:10). When he sniffs out our interest in dangerous desires, he prowls around us with great intentionality. He doesn't know our thoughts, but he can certainly see when we start entertaining sinful possibilities and flirting with compromise.

Her emotions were so deeply entangled with another man that she felt as if she would die without him. But at the same time the weight of guilt and shame was slowly squeezing the life out of her. She felt utterly destroyed, trapped, and miserable.

Sin is such a lie. It promises to fill the gaps of our disappointments with satisfaction. In reality, it just goes straight to our hearts and fills them with shame. If only we could see from the outset what the choice of sin will do to us. As Ravi Zacharias said, "Sin will take you farther than you want to go, keep you longer than you want to stay, and cost you more than you want to pay."[5]

Yes, sin is a lie, and its subtle suggestions are being whispered into your ears and mine right now by the one with death on his breath. But we don't have to simply sit and take it, trying our best not to listen. We can do something about it.

The thing that has helped me so much is to study exactly what the enemy wants to do to me. I've heard it said before that we shouldn't focus on the enemy. And I agree. We shouldn't focus on him, but we should fight him. And God's Word gives us powerful insights to better understand the enemy's tactics, which are very worth studying. After all, if God made sure it was written in His Word, then we need to make sure to read it and understand it. Once we do, we can be better equipped to counter the enemy's attacks.

Let's take a closer look at what the enemy wants to do to you and my friend and to me this very day:

- Tempt
- Deceive
- Accuse

Temptation

As I said, the enemy can't read our minds. However, he can study our patterns and hear our expressed disappointments. He knows our disappointments create pain and our brains demand something to ease every ache. This is a perfect doorway through which Satan can enter in with his evil enticements and temptations.

I wish every temptation had a warning label on it, so we'd know what we were getting ourselves into.

Your warning label might look like this if you're tempted to overspend:

"You will begin to look at other people's lives and see all the shiny, new things they have. It will start off as a small seed of jealousy that will grow until you rationalize that you deserve those things too. You will make an extra purchase online and bend the monthly budget just a smidge. But it won't stop there. Sin and secrecy have ravenous appetites. Before you know it, you'll be hiding credit card bills from your husband, being dishonest in your relationships, and facing a growing amount of debt. Your seemingly small decisions today will not only affect you, but they'll ultimately lead to the division and possibly destruction of your family and the peace you took for granted."

Or maybe you're tempted to gossip, and your warning label would say this:

"You will convince yourself it's okay to share one juicy detail about someone with a friend, as long as you follow it up with, 'But don't tell anyone.' Each time you divulge a secret that isn't yours to tell, you'll feel a little more accepted by the captive audience. It will feel good to be the one who knows it all. But this house of cards will quickly come crashing down as friends and family lose their trust in you. You will no longer be known as a person of integrity or credibility. Relationships will disintegrate. And the words once whispered by you about others will make their return voyage as you eventually become the one being gossiped about."

Take a second to think about this. What would the warning label in your life say?

My friend's warning label would have said something like this:

"You will think this is a way to ease the loneliness you feel. You will think it will make you feel all the things you deserve to feel: beautiful, respected, noticed, appreciated for who you are, and validated as special. You will think that you are the exception in being able to handle a flirty friendship without crossing any lines and that it won't hurt anyone. You will think this is going to be wonderful, because it stirs up such warm feelings in those places deep inside your heart that have felt cold for so long. You will think all those warm fuzzies are good for you. But it's all a lie. You are being blinded with desire. You are being made deaf to truth. You are reaching for a forbidden fruit that looks so good on the outside but is filled with razors on the inside. You can't even take a bite without getting cut. And, worst of all, even though you are bleeding from that first bite, you'll get so enamored with its alluring sweetness that you'll keep eating it. You will devour this sin without realizing it's devouring you. Trust me, your feelings are lying to you. This won't fix your disappointments. It will only multiply them into devastations."

Those warning labels are all throughout the Bible. For example, James 1:13–16 and verses 21–22 tell us:

When tempted, no one should say, "God is tempting me." For God cannot be tempted by evil, nor does he tempt anyone; but each person is tempted when they are dragged away by their own evil desire and enticed. Then, after desire has conceived, it gives birth to sin; and sin, when it is full-grown, gives birth to death.

Don't be deceived, my dear brothers and sisters . . .

Therefore, get rid of all moral filth and the evil that is so prevalent and humbly accept the word planted in you, which can save you.

Do not merely listen to the word, and so deceive yourselves. Do what it says.

But, if my Bible is collecting dust and my conscience is being hushed, then my heart is in danger of being crushed.

That's not a sing-song rhyme.

That's truth.

Temptation only works if our enemy keeps the consequences hidden from us.

The enemy is thrilled when we don't open our Bibles, and he

knows when we don't. He also knows how to attack us in that vulnerable place. But Truth sheds light on healthy ways to process our disappointments and the good things God can bring from them. If we can remember this, we can see more clearly what a horrible trap Satan's temptations really are.

The enemy wants us to think the Bible is too complicated to understand and too difficult to live out. This is nothing more than an evil marketing plan crafted in the depths of hell to sell you something you don't have to buy. Your mind was made by God; therefore, your brain is perfectly capable of receiving what it needs to receive, of reading the warning labels God has provided in His Word. And even if your brain doesn't understand some things, your soul is made by God to respond to Truth. You don't have to be a scholar. You just have to be created by God. And you are that. Therefore, you can receive God's Word, and His Word will achieve all the wonderful purposes meant for you.

> For the word of God is alive and active. Sharper than any double-edged sword, it penetrates even to dividing soul and spirit, joints and marrow; it judges the thoughts and attitudes of the heart. Nothing in all creation is hidden from God's sight. Everything is uncovered and laid bare before the eyes of him to whom we must give account.
>
> Therefore, since we have a great high priest who has ascended into heaven, Jesus the Son of God, let us hold firmly to the faith we profess. For we do not have a high priest who is unable to empathize with our weaknesses, but we have one who has been tempted in every way, just as we are—yet he did not sin. Let us then approach God's throne of grace with confidence, so that we may receive mercy and find grace to help us in our time of need. (Hebrews 4:12–16)

Remember, Satan knows how powerful God's Word is, and he wants to keep us from it. Don't let him.

Deception

God is the author of the Truth that empowers us. Satan is the author of the deception that imprisons us. And once he's isolated us and imprisoned us, his plan is to destroy us. There is no freedom in sin. There is a quickly fading thrill with sparks and fireworks, but then darkness envelopes, and you realize the party is in a prison cell.

Anything that doesn't line up with Truth is a lie. And where there is a lie, the enemy is at work. The longer he can keep someone deceived, the more their flesh will scream for pleasure, and soon they will become slaves to the most depraved versions of their desires.

> These people are springs without water and mists driven by a storm. Blackest darkness is reserved for them. For they mouth empty, boastful words and, by appealing to the lustful desires of the flesh, they entice people who are just escaping from those who live in error. They promise them freedom, while they themselves are slaves of depravity—for "people are slaves to whatever has mastered them." (2 Peter 2:17–19)

Those are hard verses. A spring without water is a spring that's dry and not fulfilling its purpose. A person like this has stopped being filled with the living water of God, grown cold and hard, and cannot fulfill the purposes of God. Instead of being grounded in Truth, they are driven by their feelings. That's how they are also like mists driven by a storm. What was just a small thought becomes part of a full-blown storm inside of them, taking over their decisions and eventually affecting those around them.

There is confusion, deception, justification, and damage that is done when we are not just being deceived by our desires but also leading others astray in the process. Whenever we are living any sort of double life, we are misleading others. We can't lead others to healthy places when we are making unhealthy choices ourselves.

But please know this is a desperate warning meant to help us, not to heap shame on us. A few verses later we are reminded that the Lord doesn't want any to perish but all to come to repentance (2 Peter 3:9).

Last week I heard my friend Levi Lusko say, "When God says 'don't' we should read it as 'Don't hurt yourself.'"

Think about that protective voice of God as we read more from His Word about the dangers of being deceived.

> Do not be deceived: God cannot be mocked. A man reaps what he sows. Whoever sows to please their flesh, from the flesh will reap destruction; whoever sows to please the Spirit, from the Spirit will reap eternal life. (Galatians 6:7–8)

But let's not just read the warnings about deception and desires. Let's read the truth of what to do with our desires.

First, we must do the honest work of admitting our motives driving the desire. Just because I want something doesn't mean it's God's best for me. Just because I can do something doesn't mean I should do it.

"'I have the right to do anything,' you say—but not everything is beneficial. 'I have the right to do anything'—but not everything is constructive" (1 Corinthians 10:23). If we are tired of waiting on God, weary from wanting something others have, aching from unresolved hurts, or desperate for some relief, we are at risk of deceiving ourselves and falling prey to the enemy's deception as well. Taking time to check our motives is crucial. I challenge myself with, "Will this make me more like Christ or less like Him?" Some other questions to ask are, "Will this help me get more healthy spiritually, emotionally, and physically?" and "Would the most spiritually mature person I know think this is a good choice?"

Next, we must know what God offers in place of unhealthy desires. Before Christ, we had desires that, though pleasurable in the moment, would lead to eventual destruction. But after we are a new creation, God's desires should become our desires. Here are a couple of verses that address this:

> As for you, you were dead in your transgressions and sins, in which you used to live when you followed the ways of this world and of the ruler of the kingdom of the air, the spirit who is now at work in those who are disobedient. All of us also lived among them at one time, gratifying the cravings of our flesh and following its desires and thoughts. Like the rest, we were by nature deserving of wrath. But because of his great love for us, God, who is rich in mercy, made us alive with Christ even when we were dead in transgressions—it is by grace you have been saved. (Ephesians 2:1–5)

> Through these he has given us his very great and precious promises, so that through them you may participate in the divine nature, having escaped the corruption in the world caused by evil desires. (2 Peter 1:4)

Now, let me admit where this might be hard for us. When our human desires are denied, they scream to be satisfied in the easiest and quickest way possible. Maybe we've sworn to ourselves that we won't get into another bad relationship, or declared that this time we will stick with the healthy eating plan. Or promised our loved ones that we will no longer make destructive choices by abusing substances. But then life happens.

We get lonely. We are suddenly desperate to feel closeness from someone even if we know that person isn't right for us. God's truth doesn't seem nearly as appealing in that moment.

We get really hungry. The cravings are intense, so the immediate gratification of a large salty order of fries feels justifiable. God's truth doesn't seem nearly as appealing in that moment.

We get overwhelmed. We just feel over it all, so numbing out seems so much more necessary than keeping a promise. God's truth doesn't seem nearly as appealing in that moment.

Trust me, I get it. I'm living the hardships that I'm talking about here in a "right now" way. That's why I can also gently but with absolute certainty say that desires gotten outside of God's best for us are hollow solutions that will only increase our loneliness, our waistband, and our pain.

God isn't shaking His finger at us; He's planning something better for us. What we are all truly desiring is more of God; His best is the only source of true satisfaction. He is the only answer to our every desire. He holds all the answers to all our disappointments and will direct our desires in His way, in His will, and in His timing. He's got a good plan for good things. He doesn't give His gifts wrapped in packages of confusion and anxiety and guilt and shame. James 1:16–17 assures us of this: "Don't be deceived, my dear brothers and sisters. Every good and perfect gift is from above, coming down from the Father of the heavenly lights, who does not change like shifting shadows."

The enemy's deception is hand-designed to draw your attention, affection, and worship away from God, the only true fulfillment of our hearts' longings. Satan rebelled against the Creator, and he wants you to do the same, to be caught in the pursuit of desires that will never satisfy. The enemy wants you to be more enamored with the pleasures of created things than the pleasure of the Creator Himself.

Remember Eve, who looked to a tree to give her wisdom, something that tree was never meant to give her? Instead of wisdom, she received the knowledge of good and evil. And having that knowledge didn't make her life better like she thought it would. She then had to carry the weight of evil that she was never meant to carry. The fruit that seemed so sweet didn't satisfy her; instead it burdened her with fear, anxiety, and shame.

These are truths that could have helped warn my friend in her situation and certainly should be glaring warning signs for anything drawing my heart away from God's best for me right now.

We all have something tugging at us.

We all do.

Being honest about that is the first step away from the enemy and back toward God. The minute we feel immune to the enemy's tactics is the minute pride, self-reliance, and self-deception rev up and God's Word gets tuned out.

Trust me, the enemy is as interested in tapping into your disappointments as he was with my friend. The enemy doesn't take vacations, so we shouldn't take vacations from studying God's Word either. We wouldn't want to go even a few hours without water, certainly not days or weeks, and we should view God's living water for our souls in the same way. Satan isn't intimidated by how strong we appear. He notices a thirsty soul quite parched. He's sneaky. He's crafty. He's subtle in how he slithers up next to us and flashes just the right thing, at just the right time, in the moments we are unknowingly weak enough to think, *Hmmm . . . that looks good. That might really satisfy me.*

It started off just that subtly with my friend. She believed the lie that it was just innocent fun. A little flirting. A few exchanges that made her feel special and unique and noticed. No worries, though, because she was in Bible study on Tuesday and in church every Sunday. Of course, she wasn't opening her Bible on her own. It was an accessory to tote along for appearances, but, honestly, she got enough from what others shared to feel adequately inspired.

She handpicked pieces and parts of what she heard in others' teachings to try to feel okay. And those verses that stood out as warnings? She deemed them harsh and for other people who had real problems.

This flirting was fine for her. She was making up for what had been so disappointing about her husband of fifteen years.

He wasn't tuned in to her needs. He was no longer intentional with his affections. He had unrealistic expectations of her and was critical when she didn't meet his needs.

She would stand in the kitchen and stare at him sitting in his office. She would narrow her gaze and think of all the many ways he fell short in her eyes. She'd asked him once about them going to counseling, and he had brushed it off, saying they didn't need that. He then encouraged her to plan another trip for them to get away and reconnect.

But the credit cards were maxed out. She rolled her eyes and turned her thoughts to someone else. He was kind. Fun. Flirty. Extravagant with gifts and had a wallet fat with money.

Never mind that he was kind, fun, and flirty with others too. And never mind that he was also married. He told her she was special to him, and she made the choice to believe him.

They could just be work friends.

Special friends.

Friends who could confide in each other about troubles at home.

They could meet for lunch.

It was a slow descent down a slippery slope. One justification after another that turned into a web of deceit. When we listen to the enemy's lies, we are prone to start telling our own lies.

A few texts a day turned into all-day dialogues.

What at once just felt like a little emotional boost now felt like an emotional lifeline. She craved more. He did too.

And it wasn't long until they were holding nothing back.

It all appeared so life-giving until one day she saw him from a distance at the mall, kissing another woman on the top of her forehead.

She was shocked. That was their special way of saying goodbye.

Daggers shot through her heart. She couldn't hold back the tears. And when she confronted him in the breakroom the next day, he blew her off. He made her feel small and slightly crazy.

The game was no longer fun.

It was a nightmare that stretched on for more than a year.

She couldn't let him go. But he wouldn't commit. And even if he would commit, deep down she felt confused and conflicted. She thought things would play out like the very best romantic movie. But you can't build something true from a pile of lies.

She'd been whispering to herself over and over, "I just need to be true to myself. To follow my heart. If it feels good, it must be good. I deserve something for me for once. After all, God wants me to be happy." But Jeremiah 17:9 clearly says our hearts can't be trusted: "The heart is deceitful above all things and beyond cure." Every single thing our emotions tell us must be held up to the Truth of God's Word. Otherwise, we will be susceptible to the way our enemy twists our thoughts and feelings and uses them to deceive us.

What my friend failed to realize was that she was being true to her most unhealthy self.

If we are going to be true to ourselves, we'd better make sure we are being true to our most surrendered, healed, and healthy selves, the ones God made us to be. A great verse to help us determine this is Psalm 19:14:

> May these words of my mouth and this meditation of my heart
> be pleasing in your sight,
> LORD, my Rock and my Redeemer.

Yes, the words of my mouth and the meditation of my heart must be pleasing to the Lord. And this can only happen when I align my words, thoughts, and desires with Scripture.

Otherwise, our desire to ease the ache of our disappointments will lead us right into the enemy's lies and his grip of destruction. We must not forget that our soul hunger can only be satisfied by daily doses of truth, otherwise we will be prone to snack on deception.

Accusation

No matter how alluring his lies are at first and how much they may seem to be rooted in your self-care, remember that Satan doesn't want to be your friend. He doesn't want to help you find happiness. He wants to accuse you.

He will use all that temptation and deception against you. When we sin we give the devil a personal script for how to make us feel unqualified and unable to be forgiven.

The worst thing that can ever happen to Satan is for us to believe that God loves us, has our best in mind, and forgives us of our sin. Why does this strike fear in Satan's heart? Why does he want to keep you trapped in sin, wallowing in deception, and having to wade through the sinking sand of accusation? Because he wants you to keep your mouth shut. Isn't it interesting that we are told in Revelation 12:10 that Satan is the one who accuses us before God all day and all night? But the very next verse teaches us that the enemy is defeated by the blood of the Lamb and the word of our testimony.

Our enemy never wants a testimony to come from our lips. Therefore, he never wants us to experience freedom, truth, and redemption. Whether or not the dust of our lives is of our own making, he never wants it to get into the hands of God.

God has a plan for our dust, but, rest assured, so does the enemy. And the enemy's plan for our dust is for it to mean nothing but destruction and death. He never wants us to see the new beginning God offers.

He wants to consume us. He wants to consume our dust, so nothing good can ever come from it.

Remember in Genesis 3:14 we read, "So the Lord God said to the serpent . . . 'on your belly you shall go, and you shall eat dust all the days of your life'" (NKJV).

This was a consequence from God, but Satan is crafty. He figured out a way to also use it as a tactic to sniff out our dust and then eat it.

Did you know that to this day snakes deliberately and purposefully eat and lick dust? I found some fascinating research that supports this verse:

> There is an organ in the roof of a snake's mouth called "Jacobson's organ." This helps the snake to smell in addition to its nose. Its darting, forked tongue samples bits of dust by picking them up on the points of the fork, which it then presents to its matching pair of sensory organs inside its mouth. Once it has "smelt" them in this way, the tongue must be cleaned so the process can be repeated immediately.
>
> Therefore serpents really *do* lick dust and eat it.[6]

I believe, just like the snakes of today, our spiritual enemy sniffs out our dust and feeds on it as well.

He wants us to see only destruction, death, and defeat. He wants his accusations to deafen us to God's promises of redemption.

This is where his gentle luring with temptation and the slow seduction of deception turns into a vicious fury of accusation. He never intended to comfort you with pleasure or coddle you with justifications. His purpose all along was to crush you with his accusations.

Here's his script:

Temptation: Don't you want to feel good? Try this . . . it's amazing.

Deception: You deserve this. You're special enough to get away with it. And no one will ever know. It will just be your well-deserved pleasure.

Accusation: Look at what you've done now. God is ashamed of you. When people find out, they will shame you and rename you as the loser you are. So you better keep it a secret. This isn't just a choice you made. This is who you really are. You'll never escape this shame or be healed of this pain. The best you can ever do is numb your pain, and I've got a few suggestions for how to do just that.

And that's how so many walk away from God's redemption and deeper into the dark cycle of temptation, deception, and accusation.

If this is where you are, consider the hope presented in 1 Peter 1:6–7 to help us understand that all we're going through—all the seasons of shattering and dust in our lives—when surrendered to the Lord can result in making our faith more genuine and bring about more praise, glory, and honor to God:

> In all this you greatly rejoice, though now for a little while you may have had to suffer grief in all kinds of trials. **These have come so that the proven genuineness of your faith**—of greater worth than gold, which perishes even though refined by fire—**may result in praise, glory and honor when Jesus Christ is revealed.** (emphasis mine)

Then verses 13–16 tell us what to do once we understand God's good plan of redemption:

> Therefore, with minds that are alert and fully sober, set your hope on the grace to be brought to you when Jesus Christ is revealed at his coming. As obedient children, do not conform

to the evil desires you had when you lived in ignorance. But just as he who called you is holy, so be holy in all you do; for it is written: "Be holy, because I am holy."

Don't be intimidated by the thought of being holy. God isn't expecting perfection. He just wants us perfectly surrendered to His way and His Word.

And finally James 5:13–16 gives us instruction of exactly what to do if we are in trouble:

> Is anyone among you in trouble? Let them pray. Is anyone happy? Let them sing songs of praise. Is anyone among you sick? Let them call the elders of the church to pray over them and anoint them with oil in the name of the Lord. And the prayer offered in faith will make the sick person well; the Lord will raise them up. If they have sinned, they will be forgiven. Therefore confess your sins to each other and pray for each other so that you may be healed. The prayer of a righteous person is powerful and effective.

I read these verses over my friend when we met, and then we prayed. I let all these truths wash deeply over my profound disappointments as well. And it helped me realize that but for the grace of God, I could be sitting where my friend was. We are all just a few poor choices away from sinful situations we never thought we'd be in.

I think my response to my friend after we studied these verses together surprised her. I looked up with tears in my eyes and whispered, "Thank you. Thank you for letting me in. Thank you for giving me reason to study all of this so intentionally. Thank you for being brave enough to let me see the danger of disappointments giving way to dangerous desires. Thank you for letting me see what the enemy never wants any of us to see: the consequences of those desires dragging us away into deadly choices. Your story will not be wasted. God is already using for good what the enemy meant for evil."

Redemption is here. Dust is being made new both for me and for you. The enemy may be vicious, but he is not victorious.

GOING *to the* WELL

If my Bible is collecting dust and my conscience is being hushed, then my heart is in danger of being crushed.

REMEMBER:

- Dangerous desires birthed inside our unsettled disappointments are nothing but a setup for a takedown.
- The enemy wants to tempt, deceive, and accuse you.
- Temptation only works if our enemy keeps the consequences hidden from us.
- Truth sheds light on darkness and helps us see what a horrible trap Satan is luring us into.
- Your soul is made by God to respond to Truth.
- God is the author of the Truth that empowers us. Satan is the author of the deception that imprisons us.
- The enemy's deception is hand-designed to draw your attention, affection, and worship away from God.
- If we are going to be true to ourselves, we'd better make sure we are being true to our most surrendered, healed, and healthy selves.
- God isn't expecting perfection. He just wants us to be perfectly surrendered to His way and His Word.
- If I forget my soul hunger can only be satisfied by daily doses of truth, I'm prone to snack on deception.
- Your story will not be wasted.

RECEIVE:

Therefore, with minds that are alert and fully sober, set your hope on the grace to be brought to you when Jesus Christ is revealed at his coming. As obedient children, do not conform to the evil desires you had when you lived in ignorance. But just as he who called you is holy, so be holy in all you do; for it is written: "Be holy, because I am holy." (1 Peter 1:13–16)

Also read:
Genesis 3:14
Psalm 18:30–32; 19:14
Jeremiah 17:9
John 10:10
1 Corinthians 10:23
Galatians 6:7–8
Ephesians 2:1–5
Hebrews 4:12–16
James 1:13–17, 21–22; 5:13–16
1 Peter 1:6–7
2 Peter 1:4; 2:17–19; 3:9
Revelation 12:10–11

REFLECT:

- If your temptations had warning labels on them, what would they say?
- What seemingly small ways are you allowing the enemy to enter your disappointments?
- Consider the three ways the enemy comes after us. Did any of these surprise you? How will you be more alert to his schemes?

Father,

I don't want to be someone the enemy can easily isolate or intimidate. A woman readily influenced by his lies and seduced by his crafty plans. I want to live this life free of his entanglements. That's why I'm so thankful for the incredible gift of Your Word. Guide me and teach me each day as I sit and read Your Truth. Let it prepare my heart and mind for battle. Enlightening and empowering me. Convicting and comforting me. Shedding light on the enemy's schemes and giving me the strength I need to stand. I declare today that while the enemy is vicious, he will not be victorious in my life. Not with You and Your truths working mightily in my heart and my life.

In Jesus' name, amen.

FIGH
WOR

TING

DS

Chapter 10

FIGHTING WORDS

I'm the queen of awkward sometimes. Especially when I get completely caught off guard and can't quite make sense of what's happening. One of the phrases Webster uses to define *awkward* is "lacking in assurance."

Yup. Nailed it.

I want to be deeply assured that my life is lining up the way I thought it would. In reality, though, my life is highly unpredictable. And when it goes off plan, as it does so often, I get flustered and unable to immediately interact with other humans in any way other than awkward.

It's not that I want to be awkward; it's just that I really, *really* like a calm sense of normalcy. I like a plan. I like things to go as planned. I like all involved to follow along with the plan. I want my people to stay within the boundary lines of safety and predictability. I don't want to experience any unexpected deviations from the plan at all, ever.

Hello, unrealistic.

Hello, invitation to getting disappointed.

Hello, awkward reaction to that disappointment.

For example, last year I had to get a colonoscopy. Without going into too much detail, that's where they put a tube with a tiny camera attached into your back door and do a little examination of your large intestine. I know and very much recognize that even the description of that is way awkward, but the experience of it is even more so. Especially if your name is Lysa TerKeurst.

I thought I knew what to expect. But my experience didn't line up with my expectation, and I felt very caught off guard by the whole ordeal. First, you cannot eat for a whole day leading up to it.

What?! And then you have to drink some crazy stuff that basically power washes your plumbing. Gross.

So, even before the procedure, I kept thinking, *You have got to be kidding me.*

When everything is all set, they put you to sleep to do the actual procedure—insert praise hands. But on very rare occasions the patient's fear or metabolism or absolute desire to be in control or something else crazy causes the patient's body to override the anesthesia, and they wake up during the procedure. Let's not psychoanalyze all that, because I am one of those people.

I woke up.

Now, of course, I don't remember waking up and didn't know I had woken up in the middle of the situation until my doctor told me the next day. That was a fun conversation. I turned all the shades of red as I slowly realized the doctor now has a new favorite story to tell whenever asked, "What was one of your most unusual #hilarious cases?"

Y'all. Supposedly, I raised my hand and said, "Excuse me, excuse me, but this isn't working for me. I'm in a bit of pain and discomfort, and I must go now."

And then I jumped off the table, grabbed at the air as if picking up my purse, and said, "Goodbye."

I can't even. What in the world?! Please say it isn't so.

The doctor calmly replied, "Well, Lysa, you might want me to remove the tube from your backside before you go. So, let's just get you back on the table for a few minutes."

As the doctor was sharing this with me the next day, he had to pause right here. He knew he wasn't supposed to laugh, so he folded his lips inside his mouth and bit down really hard until he could continue. "I've never had a patient jump off the table before. Ever."

Well then, there's that.

Like I said, I don't like getting caught off guard. And I suppose that fear is woven so deeply into the fiber of my being that even my subconscious self will react to things not going as I expected.

You might have even thought about that as we've progressed through this book. In the earlier chapters, it appears as if Art and I aren't together. At the time I wrote those chapters, we weren't together. We don't live together even as of right now, but then you read he's holding my hand and helping me walk through cancer. Then you read that there are no guarantees where we will be by the time this book is published.

I'm in a long season of life not looking like I thought it would. There is no part of me that doesn't want us to make it. I want my family together. But there are things that have to change in order for us to come back together in a healthy way. Those things take time, and everyone has to make choices that align with that.

It's all so unpredictable. And at times a bit awkward.

And I suspect with some circumstances in your life, you feel the same way. Your situations might be different, but that "unknown factor" makes things a bit awkward for you as well.

Maybe you're in a job where you feel unsettled and you think that God is leading you somewhere else, but He hasn't yet revealed what's next. So, for now, you walk into an office every day and just show up. It's awkward.

Or maybe your child has a teacher this year who is not a good fit. You've talked to the teacher, and nothing has changed. You've talked to the school, and nothing has changed. You feel weary and helpless and stuck in the middle of a situation that is constantly catching you and your child off guard.

Or maybe you've been watching everyone else in your life find love, walk down the aisle, and start the life you've dreamed of for yourself. Then a few months ago you met someone who was everything you've been hoping for. You clicked with them. You told your friends you thought this might be the one. And then this week you felt that person pulling back. It's hard to understand. You feel panicked. But the more you press in, the more distance you feel between the two of you.

There are thousands of scenarios that evoke these feelings of uncertainty, fear, and exhaustion from life not being like you thought it would be.

Whatever your situation is, you probably feel like you can't change it, but you still have to live through the realities of what's happening right now. Sometimes you just have to walk in your "I don't know."

The Lord makes it clear in His Word that things will not always go as we wish they would in this life between two gardens:

In this world you will have trouble. (John 16:33)

Each day has enough trouble of its own. (Matthew 6:34)

Dear friends, do not be surprised at the fiery ordeal that has come on you to test you, as though something strange were happening to you. (1 Peter 4:12)

All this trouble is exhausting. Walking in the "I don't know" is scary.

That's where I'm at.

And that's where we get weary and the tentacles of the fear of the unknown can have strangling effects on us.

Fear seems to be a close cousin of disappointment. They are related, because we feel them so deeply, they paralyze us so easily, and the pat answers so many Christians try to place on them trip us up. We are desperate to make things easier than they really are.

I get it.

But in this life between two gardens that's just not how most things work out. We get through one disappointment and then another comes. And another.

We get through the prep of the colonoscopy, but then we find out we jumped off the table in the middle of the procedure.

Where will this crazy train stop? I'd like to get off, please.

We all keep thinking, if we can just get through this circumstance, then life will settle down and finally the words *happily ever after* will scroll across the glorious scene of us skipping happily into the sunset.

But what if life settling down and all your disappointments going away would be the worst thing that could happen to you?

What if your "I don't know" is helping you, not hurting you?

What if your "I don't know" is helping you let go of things you aren't supposed to know, because that knowledge would be too heavy a burden for today? But the One you do know, the Lord, is so perfectly capable to bear it all.

Remember those verses we just read about troubles?

Here they are again in the context of the full passages:

"I have told you these things, so that in me you may have peace. In this world you will have trouble. But take heart! I have overcome the world." (John 16:33)

"But seek first his kingdom and his righteousness, and all these things will be given to you as well. Therefore do not worry about tomorrow, for tomorrow will worry about itself. Each day has enough trouble of its own." (Matthew 6:33–34)

"Dear friends, do not be surprised at the fiery ordeal that has come on you to test you, as though something strange were happening to you. But rejoice inasmuch as you participate in the sufferings of Christ, so that you may be overjoyed when his glory is revealed." (1 Peter 4:12–13)

The crucial detail for us to have peace in the middle of everything we face is to stay close to the Lord. Circle these words in the above passages: *in me, seek first his, participate.*

We think we want comfort in the I-don't-know times of life. But comfort isn't a solution to seek; rather, it's a by-product we'll reap when we stay close to the Lord.

> Comfort isn't a solution to seek; rather, it's a by-product we'll reap when we stay close to the Lord.

What if the comfort and certainties we crave today are a deadly recipe for complacency that will draw our hearts further and further away from God? There are many examples of this in the Bible, but let's look at one tucked into Jeremiah:

Moab has been at rest from youth, like wine left on its dregs, not poured from one jar to another—she has not gone into exile. So she tastes as she did, and her aroma is unchanged. (Jeremiah 48:11)

On the surface it may seem like the nation of Moab has it good. They are comfortable. Life seems predictable.

They've been at rest for a long time.

They've not been taken into exile.

They haven't known what it's like to get caught off guard. To suffer. To endure hardships due to circumstances beyond their control. Life feels good, so it must be good. No disappointments. No difficulties.

But this verse is very clear that this is not what's best for them.

Wine left on its dregs, not poured from one jar to another, means it's been left sitting in comfort for so long that it has absorbed the aroma of complacency. Winemakers at the time of Jeremiah would pour wine from jar to jar for two reasons. First, so the wine wouldn't absorb the flavor of the vessel. And second, to rid the wine of the dregs or the sediment that would settle into the bottom and prevent the wine from being pure.

The Moabites were not jarred from their complacency. Therefore, their culture was saturated with satisfaction apart from the Lord, and their people were full of impurities. They had no need to draw upon the Lord's strength, so their hearts were far from Him.

The Moabites were lulled into a false sense of security. Without challenges and changes people tend to grow increasingly distant from God and resistant to His ways.

The Moabites lived in a place geographically where they escaped the invasion of the Syrians and Babylonians who came in to destroy Israel. The Moabites were untouched. Because they were untouched, they could settle into complacency while their neighbors, the Israelites, were forced to depend on God and to learn to survive suffering, captivity, enslavement. The Israelites appear to be the ones not being "saved" from hardship by God. But if we look through the lens of what's best in the long term, Israel was being strengthened by God for its eventual good.

Settling into complacency might seem to be comfortable for today, but in the long run we, like the Moabites, may suffer more if we go untouched by God for too long.

Make no mistake: being lulled into a false sense of security is worse than going through the process of suffering.

It would have been better for the Moabites to go through the experience of the Israelites. To go from vessel to vessel and experience suffering in doses that made them strong enough to handle suffering in even larger doses.

It's like getting a colonoscopy just to make sure you catch something wrong in its early stages while treatment is possible. Or like getting a vaccine before going on a missions trip to a country where diseases are an everyday risk. It's so much better to get a small exposure to the deadly disease to help build up your immunity than to be exposed and risk not having the necessary strength and immunities to fight it.

We must sip the suffering of today, so we don't have to drown in the devastations of tomorrow.

Just as we have to get off the couch and pour ourselves into working out if we want to gain physical strength, we have to be poured into circumstances that will result in our being transformed if we want to gain spiritual strength. In the middle of our disappointments and hard times, we must seek to be transformed into thinking biblically, processing with truth instinctively, and trusting God implicitly.

We must get rid of the dregs—weakness, fear, complacency, and the hopeless resignation that all of life is unfair and God is unjust. To sit in those dregs will cause us to absorb more and more of the world's way of thinking. To think like the world leads to death—death of hope, death of peace, death of joy. But to think like Christ is to have fresh life breathed inside of us and His peace radiating from us.

Those who live according to the flesh have their minds set on what the flesh desires; but those who live in accordance with the Spirit have their minds set on what the Spirit desires. The mind governed by the flesh is death, but the mind governed by the Spirit is life and peace. (Romans 8:5–6)

To be poured out into new vessels may seem uncomfortable, chaotic, and completely unfair in the moment, but it's our only hope of seeing what God wants us to see and trusting Him in it. This is what Jesus did. This is what Jesus modeled. To be like Jesus, we must become more and more saturated with Him and less and less saturated with our human ways of processing circumstances.

We must not go too long untouched by God.

If we want to know God's will, God's perspective, God's good that He has in store for us, then we must not be conformed to the world's way of processing life but be transformed by God's Word and God's way: "Do not conform to the pattern of this world, but be transformed by the renewing of your mind. Then you will be able to test and approve what God's will is—his good, pleasing and perfect will" (Romans 12:2).

When we ask for God's strength, peace, courage, and the ability to overcome and to right the wrongs, God will pour us into circumstances He knows will infuse us with the very things we've asked Him to give us. It's good for us to desire these maturing qualities. And it's good for God to give them to us. The process of acquiring these good qualities doesn't usually feel good at the time, but it will be good in time.

So, what about the Moabites?

The following verses describe their eventual doom:

We have heard of the glories of Moab, of its excessive pride and its boasting, of its outbursts of false propaganda. For this shall the Moabites *be made to* lament, and all *have cause to* bewail Moab: they shall groan at the ruin of Kir Hareseth in utter dejection . . . The joyful festivity will be gone from the orchards; no shouts of delight shall sound in the vineyards. The wine treaders will tread no wine in the presses; the vintage shout I will bring to an end. (Isaiah 16:6–7, 10 IIT)

And what about the Israelites? They were far from perfect. But their hard times were their close-to-God times. Their disappointments became divine appointments. Because when they were desperate for God, they remained with God. And those were the times when they would experience great blessing, joy, and peace.

Isaiah 43:1–5 (AMP) gives us such a joyous glimpse of God redeeming His people. In this season, they did not go untouched by God. He held them and helped them and delivered them. And He will do the same for us!

> But now, this is what the LORD, your Creator says, O Jacob,
> And He who formed you, O Israel,
> "Do not fear, for I have redeemed you [from captivity];
> I have called you by name; you are Mine!
>
> "When you pass through the waters, I will be with you;
> And through the rivers, they will not overwhelm you.
> When you walk through fire, you will not be scorched,
> Nor will the flame burn you.
>
> "For I am the LORD your God,
> The Holy One of Israel, your Savior;
> I have given Egypt [to the Babylonians] as your ransom,
> Cush (ancient Ethiopia) and Seba [its province] in exchange
>   for you.

"Because you are precious in My sight,
You are honored and I love you,
I will give *other* men in return for you and *other* peoples in
exchange for your life.

"Do not fear, for I am with you."

Every time we face anything that causes us to cry out to God, let's declare that this hard time will be a holy time, a close-to-God time.

And if the people you love are going through a hard time, I want you to declare this same thing for them. This hard time will be a holy time! A close-to-God time!

These disappointments we all go through are actually divine appointments to see God do a new thing. Pouring us out of the old wine jars that have kept us in stale thinking and into the new jars of minds transformed by Christ's perspective.

Isaiah 43:18–19 reminds us, "Forget the former things; do not dwell on the past. See, I am doing a new thing! Now it springs up; do you not perceive it? I am making a way in the wilderness and streams in the wasteland."

We were not made to dwell in the past but instead to abide—to soak in and be saturated—with Christ in the present.

And here's the amazing thing. As I've been poured out from jar to jar, from hard time to hard time, from disappointment to disappointment, I've finally realized what the dregs were and why it was so crucial I get rid of them. They are the very things that trouble me and depress me—the wrong understandings of what I'm going through.

If we have a misunderstanding of God, we will most certainly have a wrong understanding of our circumstances.

But when we see that God's purpose is good, we can trust His process is good.

When we are poured out and purified, other situations that arise won't bother us the way they used to. Disappointments won't sting the way they used to. Hurts won't dig in so deeply the way they used to. We won't get discouraged and derailed the way we used to.

We won't get nearly as caught off guard when we trust that God is on guard looking to strengthen us for what He sees coming. "God will strengthen you with his own great power so that you will not give up when troubles come, but you will be patient" (Colossians 1:11 NCV).

Then, when the next hard circumstance comes, we'll realize it doesn't affect us as much as it would have last year. We are being changed. Our thoughts are being rearranged. And we will thank God He didn't let us just stay the same.

So back to my colonoscopy. No part of that procedure is ever fun. But it helps doctors see what they need to see, so they can know what they need to know, and therefore do what they need to do. It's not to make us suffer; it's to keep us healthy, and possibly even save our lives.

The doctors know things we don't know. And on an even more crucial level, so does God.

I don't want to leave this chapter without equipping you with some powerful Bible verses to declare as you trust God with everything you are facing and will face. Psalm 145:18 assures us that "The Lord is near to all who call on him, to all who call on him in truth."

That truth part is crucial! When we express God's truth, we depress the enemy's lies. And as I did some more research on what parts of us are most vulnerable to being controlled by those lies, I came up with this list. The enemy tries to gain a foothold over:

Affection—my heart, what I love
Adoration—my mouth, what I worship
Attention—my mind, what I focus on
Attraction—my eyes, what I desire
Ambition—my calling, what I spend my time seeking
Action—my choices, how I stand firm

So, at the end of this chapter I want to equip you with scriptures for every one of these areas.

My friend Ellie Holcomb calls reciting Scripture over every vulnerable place and situation we face our "fighting words." She has an amazing song by that title that declares:

Fight the lies with the truth, oh-ohh
Keep my eyes fixed on You
I will sing the truth into the dark
I will use my fighting words.

This isn't just a great song. Using God's truth as your fighting words will not change **what** you see, but it absolutely will change **how** you see.

I had to do this just a few days ago.

As I was returning home from getting a second opinion on my cancer diagnosis, I saw a girl on the plane crying. She didn't even try to stop the wet streams down her face. It was as if her heart had so much overload that it just overflowed out of her eyes, down past her jawbone, and splattered right onto her lap.

I didn't have to ask her what was wrong.

I knew.

I was staring at my own reflection in the plane window.

She was me.

Me slipping into that place where the tears might never stop. They'd formed a river and threatened to drown me in despair. But as Lamentations 3:21–23 reminds us, we are to call in the hope by recalling the truth:

> Yet this I call to mind
> and therefore I have hope:
>
> Because of the LORD's great love we are not consumed,
> for his compassions never fail.
> They are new every morning;
> great is your faithfulness.

I needed some fighting words. Because in that moment I was not really happy about being poured into yet another hard disappointment. But I knew if I started declaring truth, my perspective would eventually catch up and my tears could then dry up. For a few minutes at least. At least enough for me not to snot on the people around me, for heaven's sake. I didn't want anyone else to have a story about me. The colonoscopy doctor's tale is quite enough—thank you very much and have a nice day!

So here you go . . . some fighting words for when you are being poured out, caught off guard, or just generally exhausted by one too many trips on the crazy train of hard disappointments.

Using God's *truth* as your fighting words will not change what you see, but it absolutely will change how you see.

When you're living in your "I don't know," the Holy Spirit will make known to you the things the Father knows will help you.

"I have much more to say to you, more than you can now bear. But when he, the Spirit of truth, comes, he will guide you into all the truth. He will not speak on his own; he will speak only what he hears, and he will tell you what is yet to come. He will glorify me because it is from me that he will receive what he will make known to you. All that belongs to the Father is mine. That is why I said the Spirit will receive from me what he will make known to you." (John 16:12–15)

Fighting Words

Affection—my heart, what I love

- I love the Lord and I know He loves me. I'm declaring today over my situation that He will rescue me; He will protect me, because I acknowledge His name. I can rest assured that when I call on Him, He will answer me. When Satan tries to isolate me, I will remember that with the Lord, I'm never alone. He promises He will be with me, deliver me, and honor me in the midst of my most troubled seasons. So I'm holding tight to these promises right now and believing them for my life.

"Because he loves me," says the LORD, "I will rescue him;
   I will protect him, for he acknowledges my name.
He will call on me, and I will answer him;
   I will be with him in trouble,
   I will deliver him and honor him."

(Psalm 91:14–15)

- The Lord has given me a heart to know Him, to declare that He *is* Lord. In this moment, I'm directing my whole heart, my affections, to align with and live out these truths. I am His, and He *is* my God, the Lord over all. Over all my disappointments, the pain, and the unknowns. With this assurance tucked into my heart, I can move forward and know that I am held by Him.

> "I will give them a heart to know me, that I am the LORD. They will be my people, and I will be their God, for they will return to me with all their heart." (Jeremiah 24:7)

- I declare right now that I will not fear bad news or hard things that I may face. They do not have any control over my heart or my relationship with Jesus. Instead, I will cling to God's Truth, which never changes with the news I receive. Truth is what I will build the foundation of my life upon! Yes, my heart belongs to the Lord and I fully trust in Him, even when my feelings beg me to doubt His goodness. Feelings don't have the final say; Truth absolutely does.

> They will have no fear of bad news;
>   their hearts are steadfast, trusting in the LORD.
>   (Psalm 112:7)

Adoration—my mouth, what I worship

- My greatest desire is for the words of my mouth and the meditation of my heart to be pleasing in the sight of the Lord. To represent the things He's doing in me, for me, and through me. I don't want my words or my thoughts to be in alignment with the enemy. So I surrender every imagined thought and spoken word over to Jesus who can redeem them and be the true center of my adoration. Nothing will ever hold a higher place in my life than the Lord—my Rock and my Redeemer.

> May these words of my mouth and this meditation of my heart
> be pleasing in your sight,
> LORD, my Rock and my Redeemer.
>
> (Psalm 19:14)

- There are many hours, days, months, and years that make up my seasons of suffering. Sometimes it feels unbearable. But I'm reminded that God cares so intimately about me that He has placed wisdom in His Word to guide me through these times of disappointment. Truth tells me that I can pray! So I lift up my raw emotions and honest struggles to the One who knows every intimate detail of my situation. And when I'm cheerful, Truth tells me to sing praises! So I lift up my voice to worship my God, in every season, for He has been so good to me.

> Is anyone among you suffering? *Then* he must pray. Is anyone cheerful? He is to sing praises. (James 5:13 NASB)

- I will worship the Lord with all my heart to elevate my love for Him and deflate any affection I have for idols in my life. Only the Lord is faithful and worthy of my praise. He has shown me unfailing love and strengthened me in His name! Satan's lies and temptations for me to adore other things are no match for the love I have received from the Lord. For the rest of my days, I choose to exalt the Lord and sing of His ways. He alone has saved me by His right hand, and I will glorify Him in all that I say and do.

> I will praise you, LORD, with all my heart;
> before the "gods" I will sing your praise.
> I will bow down toward your holy temple
> and will praise your name
> for your unfailing love and your faithfulness,
> for you have so exalted your solemn decree
> that it surpasses your fame.
> When I called, you answered me;
> you greatly emboldened me. . . .
>
> Though I walk in the midst of trouble,
> you preserve my life.
> You stretch out your hand against the anger of my foes;
> with your right hand you save me.
>
> (PSALM 138:1–3, 7)

Attention—my mind, what I focus on

- Life may be swirling all around me, threatening to steal my hope, my peace, my joy. But I am declaring right now that I will *not* be swept up into a storm of fear and wild emotions. The Lord has promised me that He will keep me in perfect peace when I fix my mind on Him. I very much recognize I will steer where I stare. So I must watch what I fixate on. If I keep staring at the wrong things, I'll go in wrong directions. I am choosing to place my attention on the Lord in this very moment. I am choosing to focus on trusting Him and believing His promises. And as I steer my attention more and more toward Him, His peace will come and flood my heart and settle my anxious mind.

> You will keep in perfect peace
>> those whose minds are steadfast,
>> because they trust in you.
>
> (ISAIAH 26:3)

- My enemy, the devil, is prowling and roaring and looking to devour me right now. He is vicious, but he will not be victorious in my life. I am declaring today that I will *not* be one of his victims, nor will I be afraid. Instead, I will be a woman who is awake and alert. A woman who—with God's help—thinks clearly, chooses wisely, and lives according to His ways. By His Word, the Lord is making me wiser than my enemy. And I know my God is keeping me safe today.

> Be alert and of sober mind. Your enemy the devil prowls around like a roaring lion looking for someone to devour.
> (1 Peter 5:8)

- I know that what consumes my mind controls my life. And I am declaring today that I will not be a woman controlled by the lies of the enemy or by my own doubts and fears. I am a woman who is choosing to listen to God's wisdom and tune her ear to His Word. Where the enemy wants to steal my focus and flood my heart with fear, I am purposefully choosing to tune him out. God's voice, spoken clearly through His Word, is the one I'm listening to today. He will help me make sound judgments. He will give me the ability to speak with wisdom and knowledge. He will guide and direct me in all that I say and do, no matter what may come my way.

> My son, pay attention to my wisdom,
>> turn your ear to my words of insight,
> that you may maintain discretion
>> and your lips may preserve knowledge.

(Proverbs 5:1–2)

Attraction—my eyes, what I desire

- The enemy would love to distract, derail, and destroy me today. But I am choosing to fix my eyes on the Lord and the path of integrity that He has chosen for me. With the Lord by my side, I *am* a woman of courage. A woman who considers her choices carefully and thinks before she acts. I will not turn to the left or to the right, blindly following paths that will lead to my destruction. Instead, I will be a woman who stays in step with the Lord, knowing that He will keep my ways steadfast and sure.

> Let your eyes look directly ahead [toward the path of moral courage]
> And let your gaze be fixed straight in front of you [toward the path of integrity].

> Consider well *and* watch carefully the path of your feet,
> And all your ways will be steadfast *and* sure.

Do not turn away to the right nor to the left [where evil may
lurk];
Turn your foot from [the path of] evil.

(Proverbs 4:25–27 AMP)

- Today, I am declaring I am not turning back or giving up.
The Lord has brought me so far, changing me and helping
me. I'm on the right track with Him, and I am going to keep
on giving Him my all! I will not live with my eyes fixed on
earthly things, following the ways of this world and being
ruled by my own appetites. I was made for more! I am a citi-
zen of high heaven! I am awaiting the arrival of my Savior.
My Jesus. The One who will transform this tired earthly
body of mine into a glorious body like His own. He will
make me beautiful and whole. He is not done with me, and
I am not done living for Him!

> So let's keep focused on that goal, those of us who want
> everything God has for us. If any of you have something
> else in mind, something less than total commitment, God
> will clear your blurred vision—you'll see it yet! Now that
> we're on the right track, let's stay on it.
>
> Stick with me, friends. Keep track of those you see run-
> ning this same course, headed for this same goal. There are
> many out there taking other paths, choosing other goals,
> and trying to get you to go along with them. I've warned you
> of them many times; sadly, I'm having to do it again. All they
> want is easy street. They hate Christ's Cross. But easy street
> is a dead-end street. Those who live there make their bellies
> their gods; belches are their praise; all they can think of is
> their appetites.

But there's far more to life for us. We're citizens of high heaven! We're waiting the arrival of the Savior, the Master, Jesus Christ, who will transform our earthy bodies into glorious bodies like his own. He'll make us beautiful and whole with the same powerful skill by which he is putting everything as it should be, under and around him. (Philippians 3:15–21 THE MESSAGE)

- The enemy would love for me to get caught up in the temptations of this world. He would love for me to give in to the devastating pull of my constant cravings for physical pleasure. The insatiable longing for all that I see. The pride that comes with achieving and owning more and more. But I declare that I am onto him and his ways. I know that pursuing pleasures outside the will of God is not what's best for me. These pleasures may feel good now but will eventually hurt me. Wrongly obtained pleasures will lead me to a place of dissatisfaction, depression, and destruction. So I'm choosing to turn to Jesus with every longing in my heart. I declare that I am not powerless in the face of great temptation. The Lord is the One who makes me strong. And He is the One who satisfies my soul.

For everything in the world—the lust of the flesh, the lust of the eyes, and the pride of life—comes not from the Father but from the world. (1 John 2:16)

Ambition—my calling, what I spend my time seeking

- As a woman who shares in the heavenly calling, who recognizes Jesus as my apostle and high priest, I declare I will pursue the purposes for which God created me. I will be most satisfied when I am most settled in my calling. I may not know all the details of the big calling before me, but I will absolutely be on assignment for God today. I will notice others who need the same kind of comfort God has given me for my hurts and disappointments, and I will offer help and hope to them. In fulfilling my assignments for today, I will most certainly discern His purposes for my future. The more I focus on Him, the more I will know His plans. He alone is worthy of my gaze and able to redeem my every thought and my every step from here.

> Therefore, holy brothers and sisters, who share in the heavenly calling, fix your thoughts on Jesus, whom we acknowledge as our apostle and high priest. (Hebrews 3:1)

- Sometimes I forget I'm not alone in my struggle. Those who have gone before me are cheering me on in the heavenly places. This reminds me to keep going, drop the weights that are getting me down, and not lose sight of Jesus, who never took His eyes off His mission to glorify God with His life on earth. Today I claim my place in the race and commit to persevere.

> Do you see what this means—all these pioneers who blazed the way, all these veterans cheering us on? It means we'd better get on with it. Strip down, start running—and never quit! No extra spiritual fat, no parasitic sins. Keep your eyes on *Jesus*, who both began and finished this race we're in. Study how he did it. Because he never lost sight of where he was headed—that exhilarating finish in and with God—he

could put up with anything along the way: Cross, shame, whatever. And now he's *there*, in the place of honor, right alongside God. (Hebrews 12:1–2 THE MESSAGE)

- I am God's masterpiece—His handiwork, created in Christ Jesus to do the good things He prepared for me to do. I declare on this day that I will see the things that come my way as God's perfect plan to develop my character to match my calling. I will walk in His ways for me and give Him praise for the way He made me for the rest of my days.

For we are God's handiwork, created in Christ Jesus to do good works, which God prepared in advance for us to do. (Ephesians 2:10)

Action—my choices, how I stand firm

- I confess that there are many days when I buy into the lie that I am helpless and hopeless. But today I am declaring hope and truth over my life. I have been equipped and blessed with the precious and powerful Word of God. His Word is steady and sure. I can stand firm on it and hold fast to it. I can keep moving forward, today and every day, as God's very breath on the page breathes fresh hope and life into me. Yes. I am loved by God and well-equipped by God. And I am choosing today to fix my eyes on His Word, fill my heart with the hope I have in Him, and let the love and grace of His Son Jesus Christ strengthen and encourage me for all He has called me to do.

So then, brothers and sisters, stand firm and hold fast to the teachings we passed on to you, whether by word of mouth or by letter. May our Lord Jesus Christ himself and God our Father, who loved us and by his grace gave us eternal encouragement and good hope, encourage your hearts and strengthen you in every good deed and word. (2 Thessalonians 2:15–17)

- I admit I spend my time anxious and worried when I should be spending my days thanking God instead. Today will be the day I give thanks rather than fall into worry. Today will be the day I pray about what is aching within me. And today will be the day I receive the peace of God that was always intended to reside within me. I will keep my mind on the things that are true, honorable, worth respect, right, biblical, pure, admirable, and good for me. For the rest of my days I will dwell on the excellent and praiseworthy, keeping these things close to my heart.

Therefore, my fellow believers, whom I love and long for, my delight and crown [my wreath of victory], in this way stand firm in the Lord, my beloved . . . Do not be anxious *or* worried about anything, but in everything [every circumstance and situation] by prayer and petition with thanksgiving, continue to make your [specific] requests known to God. And the peace of God [that peace which reassures the heart, that peace] which transcends all understanding, [that peace which] stands guard over your hearts and your minds in Christ Jesus [is yours]. Finally, believers, whatever is true, whatever is honorable *and* worthy of respect, whatever is right *and* confirmed by God's word, whatever is pure *and* wholesome, whatever is lovely *and* brings peace, whatever is admirable *and* of good repute; if there is any excellence, if there is anything worthy of praise, think *continually* on these things [center your mind on them, and implant them in your heart]. (Philippians 4:1, 6–8 AMP)

- Whenever I get lost in what feels too hard and my thoughts start to veer off into an unhealthy place, I will remember God is unchanging, always true, and never fails to follow through on His promises to me. He is never late, never untrustworthy, and loves me more than I could begin to comprehend. He is to be trusted, and I will rest in Him.

  God is not human, that he should lie, not a human being, that he should change his mind. Does he speak and then not act? Does he promise and not fulfill? (Numbers 23:19)

When we declare these fighting words and live them out, we will be strengthened. Confident. And ready to fight Satan's vicious lies with the powerful truth of God's Word.

GOING *to the* WELL

Comfort isn't a solution to seek; rather it's a by-product we'll reap when we stay close to the Lord.

REMEMBER:

- Being lulled into a false sense of security is worse than going through the process of suffering.
- To be like Jesus, we must become more and more saturated with Him and less and less saturated with our human ways of processing circumstances.
- These disappointments we all go through are actually divine appointments to see God do a new thing.
- If we have a misunderstanding of God, we will most certainly have a wrong understanding of our circumstances.
- When we express God's truth, we depress the enemy's lies.
- Using God's truth as your fighting words will not change *what* you see, but it absolutely will change *how* you see.

RECEIVE:

God will strengthen you with his own great power so that you will not give up when troubles come, but you will be patient. (Colossians 1:11 NCV)

Also read:
Numbers 23:19
Psalm 19:14; 91:14–15; 112:7; 138:1–3, 7; 145:18
Proverbs 4:25–27; 5:1–2
Isaiah 16:6–7, 10; 26:3; 43:1–5, 18–19
Jeremiah 24:7; 48:11
Lamentations 3:21–23
Matthew 6:33–34
John 16:12–15, 33
Romans 8:5–6; 12:2
Ephesians 2:10
Philippians 3:15–21; 4:1, 6–8
2 Thessalonians 2:15–17
Hebrews 3:1; 12:1–2
James 5:13
1 Peter 4:12–13; 5:8
1 John 2:16

REFLECT:

- What if your "I don't know" is helping you, not hurting you? Even now, what positives can you see coming from your season of disappointment?
- What comforts and certainties are you craving right now that could possibly result in complacency down the road, drawing your heart further away from God?
- We all need to have some fighting words on hand so we can declare God's truth over our difficult situations. Which declaration at the end of this chapter spoke to your heart and circumstance the most?

Father,

I want to look more and more like You. I want to think more and more like You. I want to act like I've spent more and more time with You. Pour me out of the dregs of wrong thinking, wrong processing, and wrong reactions. Pour me into circumstances that make me desperate for Your touch. I want to conform to You, so I can be transformed by absorbing Your essence. I believe You. I trust You. Make me more like You, I pray.

In Jesus' name, amen.

UPSIDE

DOWN

Chapter 11
UPSIDE DOWN

Just so you know, I wish I could take away every disappointment that nips at the edges of your happiness and sits heavy in your heart. Big and small. A past hurt or a present heartbreak. I wish we could get together in the comforts of my white kitchen with dishes in the sink and laundry on the table needing to be folded. I'd offer you some warm slice-and-bake cookies and whisper, "I get it. Let's chat."

I could share my stuff, and you could share yours.

We'd probably cycle through stories of the smaller craziness of life first. Like the time my makeup got mixed up with my daughter's. No big deal; I'm flexible enough to use hers. The lighting wasn't very good where I was doing my makeup, so it all looked fine.

Until later at the office.

I walked into our brightly lit restroom and just about keeled over. My. Eyebrows. Were. Purple! That was no eyebrow pencil I'd used hours earlier. It was purple eyeliner. People had been interacting with me all day saying not a word. Gracious.

Or the time I convinced myself that the really adorable shirt on sale could fit me. I mean, I knew the tag said it was two sizes too small, but where there's a will there's a way. Right? Well, not so much. I got stuck. My arms were up and too far committed when I suddenly realized I couldn't move. My face was covered with the body of the shirt; therefore, I also couldn't see. My little muffin top was the only thing free as a bird as I was forced to walk out into the store blindly and squeak out, "Um, I need a little help."

Why do these things keep happening to me?

Once we'd had a laugh together, we'd get to the deeper issues. The bigger disappointments. The harder things to process.

And we'd both agree this isn't how it should be. This life between two gardens is confusing and complicated. Dust is messy.

We don't even like to touch dust, especially if it's made up of the shattered pieces of our own hearts.

Thankfully, we don't have to. We can hand it over to God—the One who forms our dust into something we want but never could have made for ourselves.

We'd nod in agreement at this thought.

I'd then share a couple of verses that have really helped me. But I would warn you, the first might not at all feel good at first glance. But it's better to wrestle with Truth than wallow in turmoil. So, I would turn to the book of James, chapter 1. I'd recite verses 2–4 from memory, which should reassure you. I've personally wrestled through turmoil with this Truth more than just a time or two.

> Consider it pure joy, my brothers and sisters, whenever you face
> trials of many kinds, because you know that the testing of your
> faith produces perseverance. Let perseverance finish its work
> so that you may be mature and complete, not lacking anything.
> (James 1:2–4)

I'd confess I like these verses until I don't. They are easy to pull out when your worst issue is that the drive-through coffee joint got your order wrong today. They frappeed your latte and waylaid the start of your workday. Grrrrrrr. But then you put a little Jesus on it and felt way mature as you considered some joy up in there.

But what about those other things we walk through? The ones that hurt too long? Or disappoint too deeply? Or feel devastatingly permanent?

To slap some "we should be joyful about this" verses on top of the hard things feels cruel. Like a bad joke about something excruciatingly painful. It's just too soon for that kind of nonsense.

That's why I'm glad these verses don't say "feel the joy" but, instead, "consider where some glimpses of joy might be even in the midst of all the hurt."

I'd share with you about my friend Angie. Maybe we could even call her in. She's a beautiful soul held together by equal amounts of belly laughs and serious sorrow. Her baby Audrey went from womb to heaven in a matter of minutes. There would be no tea parties with her sisters. No secrets shared with her best friends. No birthday parties or Build-A-Bear outings with her daddy.

Just a sweet legacy that she fulfilled her assignment here quicker than most and got to make all those memories with Jesus.

But her momma weeps for her still. Angie's arms ache to hold her, and her eyes long to see Audrey grow.

It was just before Audrey's ninth birthday when I got a text from Angie that a painting I'd commissioned an artist friend to do for Proverbs 31 Ministries took her breath away. Angie had seen it on social media, and it looked so much like she imagined Audrey looking now at nine. There were details in the painting that the artist could have never known to include except through divine inspiration. Angie wept at the sight.

The problem was that the painting had already been sold.

So, her husband, Todd, and I contacted the artist who, with even more precision, created another original for Angie. Just before Todd surprised Angie with a visit to the studio to get her treasure, I sent Deann, the artist, a note to scribble on the back from me. It read,

> Dearest Angie,
>
> Audrey isn't forgotten. And neither are you. God wanted you to have a picture of your beautiful nine-year-old daughter to assure you she's good. You will see her again. But, until then, here

she is. Beautiful. Whole. So proud of her mommy. God shows up in amazing ways. Today it's through Deann's paintbrush.

I love you,

Lysa

At this point in our conversation, I'd pull up Angie's Instagram and show you what she wrote in response. It so deeply comforted me. Her words gave me such hope in the midst of my own heartbreak. Because sometimes when you can't find your footing with your own faith, you just have to go stand on someone else's for a while.

She wrote:

> The kindness of the Lord is more than I can begin to comprehend.
>
> Genuinely, one of the best days of my life. I will never, ever forget the way Lysa wrote a dedication on the back for Audrey . . . and Deann's brushes painted life into my angel.
>
> I'm overwhelmed. So many tears of gratitude.
>
> ❤ Thank you, Lord. . . . I'm going to post more photos so y'all can see it better—it is so, so spectacular. I'm completely in awe.

She said she was spilling *tears of gratitude*. Dare I say that's one of the best descriptions I've ever heard of what it is to consider the presence of joy in the middle of an unimaginable disappointment?

She gets it.

To live is to love. To love is to risk pain. To risk pain is to live. It's what it means to truly be human. As fragile as dust. The breaking of us. The making of us. The building up of our faith.

Tears are the truest connection we have with others, and trust is the truest connection we have with God. Angie's tears of gratitude touched a deep part of me and helped me to think with a heart of gratitude and trust as I wrestled with my own tears.

And doesn't it all come down to that? Trust. Trading our will for "Thy will," because we know He will.

Understanding how to consider it all pure joy rises and falls on whether we truly trust God in the middle of what our human minds can't see as good at all. It's hard. So I like to think of it in terms of baking. Imagine today if we decided to make a cake.

Not like "I went to the store and bought one from their bakery to stick on my cake plate and just smiled when people commented on my masterpiece." Not that.

Instead, one where we bought all the right ingredients from the store and used them for a from-scratch recipe.

After going to the store, we set out all the ingredients: the flour, the butter, the sugar, the vanilla, the eggs, the baking powder, and a pinch of salt. But then maybe we felt too tired to mix it all together and make the cake. Instead we thought we could just enjoy the cake one ingredient at a time. The thing is that sometimes we don't like some of the individual ingredients, so we'd rather leave them out.

The flour is too dry—leave it out.

The sugar, butter, and vanilla are all good—leave them in!

The eggs are just gross when raw—definitely leave those out!

And then our cake would never be made mature and complete, not lacking anything.

We are so quick to judge the quality of our lives and the

Trust.

Trading our will

for "Thy will,"

because we

know He will.

reliability of God based on individual events rather than the eventual good God is working on putting together.

We must know that just like the master baker has reasons to allow the flour and eggs in right measure into his recipe, Jesus, the author and perfecter of our faith, will do the same with dry times and hard times. And yes, we may have to go through some chaos in the mixing and some heat in the baking, but soon we will rise and live lives that are a sweet offering of hope, grace, peace, and comfort to others.

That's how we can consider it pure joy today. There's purpose in the pain and joy in the making of a life with Jesus.

James goes on to show us what we can set our eyes on as we persevere in this joy:

> Blessed is the one who perseveres under trial because, having stood the test, that person will receive the crown of life that the Lord has promised to those who love him. (James 1:12)

Oh, can you imagine? Being deemed worthy to receive a crown of life? Remember how they placed a crown of thorns on Jesus? What a picture of how our sorrows feel today—so much like a crown of thorns. But that awful crown is a foreshadowing of how eternity will change everything. It will all be turned upside down in eternity. Grief will turn to joy. Heartbreak to shouts of thanksgiving. Crowns of thorns to crowns of gold fit for a king.

I did a little research on this crown of life. This crown will be given to those called into special service to the King because of their dedication to Him. Their hearts may have been broken during their earthly lives, but their spirits never were. They trusted Jesus and loved Jesus and cared for people all the way through. But instead of wallowing in pity, they just kept letting Jesus turn their dust into pottery—beautiful and strong and useful for noble purposes.

And then, in keeping with their hearts being completely in love with Jesus, the minute they enter eternity and receive their crowns, many Bible scholars believe they will immediately lay them at the feet of Jesus, so thankful to have a gift to give the King.

Such a joy! Even after giving up their actual crowns, these people will continue to carry this honor bestowed upon them. They will be designated as those Jesus recognizes as His closest friends.

I could cry thinking about it.

I want to live every minute of every day considering the joy of right now and the joy of that day.

I'd whisper all of this to you as we sit together over our plate of cookies, because we are kindred spirits.

One minute we'd be sharing our stuff with words. And the next with simple tears. But our common pain wouldn't need the gaps filled or the play-by-play details given, because we'd just know.

I'd insist that we pull out small canvases and paint together. You might not want to, but I'd assure you that we needn't be so worried about painting masterpieces. People are the masterpieces, and you are creative because you are God's best creation and His fingerprints and brush strokes dance all inside of you. Then I'd hold up my written rules for paintbrush holders and clear my throat in a dramatic fashion.

- Everyone must try.
- Give yourself permission to not be perfect.
- Refuse to be intimidated by the process.
- The most beauty will emerge from the paintbrushes held by those who are most free from fear.

- Smile. I already love what will soon come to life on your canvas.

We'd relax and realize these are also good rules for life.

Then we'd paint. And you'd discover you actually like it. Your piece would turn out amazing, and together we'd think through the perfect place for you to hang it up in your house. It's a small victory for us both. We are slowly coming out of hiding. It feels good to be vulnerable with artwork and with each other.

We'd eventually pull out some coffee and probably soon need some chips and queso as well. So we'd get in the car. The music would be turned up. The windows would be rolled down. And we'd pick that cheap place where they put sombreros on red-faced souls celebrating birthdays and offer free guacamole on Tuesdays.

We'd have that messy-hair-don't-care attitude as we get lost in laughter one minute and deep thoughts the next. We'd most certainly drip salsa on our white shirts and tears on our ripped jeans.

We'd lose track of time. I'd reach over and give you a hug as I exhale and simply punctuate our discussion by saying, "Whew. All the stuff. All the stuff."

Then it would be time to head back to each of our homes. But before we parted I'd pull out my journal and read you one more thing.

It's a dialogue between God and Jesus that just spilled out from my pen to my journal one day.

It's not prophecy. Nor am I trying to proclaim divine words that aren't mine to give. But when this allegory came to me, it settled into my soul and felt right for both you and me.

I call it "Upside Down" and with a nod in your direction, I dedicate this to you.

The Son turned his head and quizzically said, "Hmmm . . . Father, those are really strange words to assign to this life. Can we pick some other words? I have some fantastic suggestions for this one. She's optimistic and strong. She's caring and compassionate. She's good and generous, and she's so very aware of others. She's a deep thinker and a deep feeler all in one. She's so very rare, Father. Yes, she's rare."

"I know. And that's why she must be upside down."

"Father, as she gets older I don't think she will like that You gave her these words. I think she will question, 'Why did You do this to me?'"

The Father replied, "She most certainly will question Me. Her favorite question of all will be 'Why?' And it will serve her well. For in the incessant wrestling she will come to learn something most people never learn. She will see I didn't do these things *to her*. I did them *for her*. Though it broke My heart to give her the opposite of what she wanted, she will watch me eventually turn all that bad into good. I will turn it all upside down, and in doing so she will live right side up. She will be a beacon of light in extreme darkness. She will be a voice of hope when others feel all is lost.

"As she learns to live in this upside-down way, she will discover there are some problems that cannot be solved, though her brain will tirelessly try. But, in the end, she will release even that—all the trying—all the wrestling to tie things up tidily. And she will finally embrace her most glorious quality of all: her messiness.

"This is the most upside-down part of the whole story. What makes her most delightful are the parts of her that are most messy. Untidy. Unpolished. Uneducated. Untouched by perfection. Untarnished by performance.

"She will effortlessly show others a way to find Me and draw their hearts into the reality that I am a good God. And most importantly that I am good at being God. No human should have to carry the weight of being their own god, but so many do.

"As she seeks Me in her mess, she will show others how to find freedom from that weight. She will be a force to be reckoned with in the great battle of good versus evil. Her gentleness will be her strength. Her love will be the fiercest weapon. Her balance will be the beauty of her soul. And her wrestling with the answers to *Why?* that never come will be her humility.

"She'll be a learner and a lover of truth. She will crave certainty. But people are unpredictable, and circumstances will often cause her confusion. So, she'll take her

uncertainties and bury them in the rich soil
of My Word.

"These will be some of our closest
times together, she and I. When she learns
something while confused—she'll remember it
forever. Truth will shape her in the best of
ways and lead her heart to want to give the
hope she's found to others. So it's through
her uncertainties she'll find her most
certain purpose in the world. She will be:

~ a *curator* of curiosity
~ an *image bearer* of imagination
~ a tender *truth-teller*
~ a bold *gospel-bringer*
~ the *wonder-full* part of *why*

"Those are the things she'll discover
as she journeys through life, dancing and
falling and getting back up again.

"But, Son, there is something you must
tell her Yourself right now today:

"Dear daughter of Mine, when the world
tries to beat that 'why' question out of you,
offer it back to the heart of every wide-
eyed inner child and whisper, 'Yes, yes,
ask away.' Because to kill that question
is to kill the passion-filled purpose that
will give you an answer. You'll never know
why that person did what they did. Or why
the seemingly perfect circumstances shifted

and corrupted the way they did. Why the destruction and devastation marched into your life. No, you'll never know those answers. But trust Me—it wouldn't make anything better even if you did have those answers. It just wouldn't. I've not kept those answers from you as a cruel exercise of My power. I've kept those answers, because only I can bear the weight of them.

"You live in a broken world where broken things happen. In a sin-soaked world *horrible* things happen. They just do. And you will hurt deeply because of these things. You, dear girl, will also watch others hurt.

"You will hear human answers that try to tie bows around the big blows of life. These sound good in a sermon but never hold up in real life. And that's when you will see what a gift it is that you've been entrusted with enough hurt to keep you humane. You'll offer the only real answer available: 'The Lord helped me survive and He'll help you too. I'll hold your hand while you find your way to Him.'

"You won't know why this and that are happening. But there is a part of the *why* you will come to know. Look around, and you will see the part of *why* I do want you to know. You'll find it in the eyes of every human you brush up against or bump into or barrel over or dare to embrace. In their eyes will be a

secret sorrow, a deep wound, a scared child.
You were made to connect with that person.
Really connect. But you'll never ever connect
with your perfections and performance. All
that's slick and shiny about you repels them
or scares them or makes them shrink back.
But your tears? Oh, they are liquid magnets
drawing others in. They are a river of
reality. A healing for hurts. A bonding for
brokenness.

"You see, it's through your tears that
people are united. It's what makes you a safe
person to others when you simply whisper, 'Me
too. Me too.'

"You won't have to bring them answers.
Just bring them your peaceful presence. And
right then and there your heart will feel
like it could just about explode with joy
that you have imperfections. They'll invite
you to stay when they realize you haven't
skipped through life untouched by failures
and faults and being made to feel fragile by
others.

"Perfection intimidates. Compassion
inspires. And in that you will finally find
the why. Why did this happen? Because there's
someone else in the world who would drown in
their own tears if not for seeing yours. And
when you make one other human simply see they
aren't alone, you make the world a better
place.

"Tell her I gave her the words *upside down* because she'll give the world permission once again to see the wonderful in the why. Her whys have made her wise.

"*Upside down* are the perfect words for a girl who will eventually land *right side up*, messy and marvelous and so very alive."

That's you, my friend. That's me. That's the remaking of dust.

GOING *to the* WELL

It will all be turned upside down in eternity. Grief will turn to joy. Heartbreak to shouts of thanksgiving. Crowns of thorns to crowns of gold fit for a king.

REMEMBER:

- It's better to wrestle with Truth than wallow in turmoil.
- To live is to love. To love is to risk pain. To risk pain is to live. It's what it means to truly be human.
- Tears are the truest connection we have with others, and trust is the truest connection we have with God.
- Trust. Trading our will for "Thy will," because we know He will.
- There's purpose in the pain and joy in the making of a life with Jesus.
- Everyone must try.
- Give yourself permission to not be perfect.
- Refuse to be intimidated by the process.
- The most beauty will emerge from the paintbrushes held by those who are most free from fear.
- No human should have to carry the weight of being their own god, but so many do.
- You will see what a gift it is that you've been entrusted with enough hurt to keep you humane.
- Perfection intimidates. Compassion inspires.

- There's someone else in the world who would drown in their own tears if not for seeing yours.
- When you make one other human simply see they aren't alone, you make the world a better place.
- Your whys have made you wise.

RECEIVE:

Blessed is the one who perseveres under trial because, having stood the test, that person will receive the crown of life that the Lord has promised to those who love him. (James 1:12)

Also read:
James 1:2–4

REFLECT:

- Would you say you have been spending more time wallowing in turmoil lately or wrestling well with Truth?
- Are there any "ingredients" in your life right now—any difficult or disappointing situations—you wish you could just leave out?
- How does knowing there is purpose in all the pain help you consider where the joy might be?
- Does the hope of the crown of life change your perspective on your suffering? How would you feel

about laying that very crown at the feet of Jesus out of a deep gratitude?

- Who do you need to share your tears with? Who needs to know they aren't alone?
- The pain and confusion often found in this life lived between two gardens can leave us feeling suspicious of God, making us wonder if He is cruel and unfair. Ask yourself, *Am I willing to believe He is protecting me and preparing me for all that is ahead?*

Father,

I've needed this look at the devastations, disappointments, and dust that seem to gather in my life. I'm tired. I'm worn. But now, I'm also hopeful. You have good plans to remake me, and I know You'll never forsake me. Your Words are true and good, and for the first time in a long time, I believe them. With everything I am, I believe them. Thank You for scooping up my shattered pieces and making them into something even better—making me into something better. For Your glory. For my good. I can't say thank You enough. Today I hand over my dust and will step back to watch You work. And as You do, I pray You would mold me more and more into the likeness of Your Son.

It is in His holy name I pray, amen.

EPILOGUE

I'm sitting on the back deck. Art reaches out to hold my hand. He's read every word of this book and nodded to say it's good. I'm honestly stunned that we're here. It's a respite that I'm equally terrified of and grateful for. What if it goes away and everything falls apart again and life implodes? Will my heart be able to withstand it? Will I feel like a fool? Will I crumble in despair?

I don't think so. Not this time.

Art and I have finally made peace with the fact we will never be more than human on this side of eternity.

I am a human who is sold out to the sacredness of marriage but who very much realizes I can't control anyone's choices but my own. I'm also a human who desperately wants to still believe love can be good. People can change. Addictions can be healed and affairs can be gotten over. It's not easy. But it's the path I'm choosing.

It's the path we are choosing.

At the same time, I have so much compassion and deep empathy for those who went a different way when placed in the same horrors and heartbreak as me. They did what they could. Oh how they cried and tried and wanted something else. I get it. And I'd be there, too, but for an unexplainable grace, a wind of change, and a man with a repentant heart letting God work in him like never before.

There is nothing I can say that I did any better or differently that helped figure this mess out. I'm as surprised as anyone. There is nothing but a broken-spined Bible, a tear-stained pillow, gut-wrenching relief, a cool breeze, and the echoes of all God's taught both of us in this life between two gardens. As I sit here in this middle place of messy humanity and divine reality, I long for this second chance to be girded with guarantees. But that's not the way it is. I'll have to step out into this new normal with eyes wide open to the fact this is risky.

To be human is to be vulnerable. It demands a trust in God that's no joke. Trusting God is the hardest lesson to learn but the most crucial.

We trust a God who allows hurt.

But we also trust a God who uses hurt for good.

Being hurt isn't the worst thing in the world. It's actually the very thing that makes us closer to Jesus and closer to our fellow humans. In a world of differences we are so very united when we simply cry together.

So I don't fear the hurt because I do trust God to bring good from it. I fear getting just comfortable enough to exhale and start reclaiming a normal that's always subject to change.

I'm exhausted by change. I still find myself resisting it. But I've been transformed into a better human because of what we've walked through. Art has too. We would have never chosen these changes but they are good. They are the hardest good we've ever lived through.

But I don't want to tie this up in a bow because real life is never that tidy. I'm still a girl who cries over what's happened, grieves what we can't get back, and gets scared. So very scared.

To open my heart again means to expose what's been so badly wounded to the sharp edge of trust again. To gain trust, you must come close. And dare to try it. Yes, this is risky. Yes, I shake with the uncertainty that it's okay to try again. Yes, I am unclear how to push away the fog of uncertainty. So, I make the choice to not try and figure it all out. I simply squeeze the hand that's offered to me and I whisper, "Okay, Art, let's try."

UPDATE FROM LYSA

Thank you for the prayers you've lifted up for me and my family in these many months since both my marriage and health announcements. Your words have carried me on days when I felt like I didn't have the strength to face the battles ahead. For that, I'm incredibly grateful.

After I finished writing the manuscript for *It's Not Supposed to Be This Way*, my doctors and I decided the best way to tackle the breast cancer would be through a double mastectomy. I underwent that surgery and, in the following weeks, was declared cancer-free. I still have several more reconstructive surgeries ahead of me but I'm so very thankful to be on my way to healing. And daily I pray for healing for others facing breast cancer and all the other scary diagnoses that make them cry.

I still don't have the answers for my "why" questions. But I have seen so many glimpses of God's faithfulness in the midst of walking through these things. And I've learned how to have a deeper trust in God even when—especially when—life doesn't make sense. That's a gift. A good gift. And one that I will cling to with much gratitude the rest of my life.

9 SCRIPTURES FOR SURVIVING THE TIMES WHEN GOD SEEMS SILENT

*A*re you desperately longing to see evidence of God moving in the midst of a heart-wrenching situation? Maybe it's the unanswered prayer you've cried countless tears over. Or the relationship you're desperate for Him to mend. Or the pain you keep asking Him to please bring to an end. I know how hard that can be.

I also know the enemy would love for you to think God is ignoring you. The truth is, God absolutely longs to help us in our hurt. But to help us, He must transform us. And all of this is because He loves us. That's why I want to highlight these three statements that are my starting place when I think about and wrestle through unmet expectations, pain, and disappointments big and small:

God longs to help me.
God longs to transform me.
God loves me.

Below you will find those statements coupled with lies we often believe and scriptures we can use to defeat those lies. When we express God's truth, we depress the lies of the enemy. I pray you will grab hold of these truths for yourself, friend. And I pray you'll rest in the knowledge that God's not ignoring you; He's restoring you.

GOD LONGS TO HELP ME

Lie:

Nothing seems to be changing. God must be ignoring my cries for help.

Truth:

> I waited patiently for the LORD;
>> he inclined to me and heard my cry.
>
> He drew me up from the pit of destruction,
>> out of the miry bog,
>
> and set my feet upon a rock,
>> making my steps secure.
>
> (Psalm 40:1–2 ESV)

I will remember:

God longs to help me, and He leans
in close to listen to me.

Lie:

I'm not sure that God notices me or cares about me. It feels like my prayers don't even matter.

Truth:

Are not two sparrows sold for a penny? And not one of them will fall to the ground apart from your Father. But even the hairs of your head are all numbered. Fear not, therefore; you are of more value than many sparrows. (Matthew 10:29–31 ESV)

I will remember:

God longs to help me, and He
cares about me deeply.

Lie:

God is probably sick and tired of me and all my weaknesses.

Truth:

Do you not know?
  Have you not heard?
The Lord is the everlasting God,
  the Creator of the ends of the earth.
He will not grow tired or weary,
  and his understanding no one can fathom.
He gives strength to the weary
  and increases the power of the weak.
(Isaiah 40:28–29)

I will remember:

God longs to help me, and His strength
is the answer for all my weaknesses.

GOD LONGS TO TRANSFORM ME

Lie:

God can't possibly change someone like me.

Truth:

For those God foreknew he also predestined to be conformed to the image of his Son, that he might be the firstborn among many brothers and sisters. (Romans 8:29)

I will remember:

God longs to transform me, and He's
making me more and more like Jesus.

Lie:

God gave up on me a long time ago.

Truth:

And I am sure of this, that he who began a good work in you will bring it to completion at the day of Jesus Christ. (Philippians 1:6 ESV)

I will remember:

God longs to transform me, and He promises
He'll complete the work He's doing in me.

Lie:

God wishes I would just hurry up and get my act together.

Truth:

For it is God who works in you, both to will and to work for his good pleasure. (Philippians 2:13 ESV)

I will remember:

God longs to transform me, and He is
the one who will help me change.

GOD LOVES ME

Lie:

I am unworthy of being loved by God.

Truth:

Very rarely will anyone die for a righteous person, though for a good person someone might possibly dare to die. But God demonstrates his own love for us in this: While we were still sinners, Christ died for us. (Romans 5:7–8)

I will remember:

God loves me, and He pursues me
even when I act unlovable.

Lie:

If God really loved me, He wouldn't let me feel this much pain.

Truth:

Consider it pure joy, my brothers and sisters, whenever you face trials of many kinds, because you know that the testing of your faith produces perseverance. Let perseverance finish its work so that you may be mature and complete, not lacking anything. (James 1:2–4)

I will remember:

God loves me, and He promises
not to waste any of my pain.

Lie:

If I'm honest with God about my feelings, He'll be disappointed and stop loving me.

Truth:

> Trust in him at all times, you people;
>> pour out your hearts to him,
>> for God is our refuge.
>
> (Psalm 62:8)

I will remember:

> God loves me, and He invites me to pour my heart out to Him honestly.

GETTING THE HELP YOU NEED

Sweet friend,

For some of you this book will be exactly what you needed to walk you through a hard season or process a deep disappointment. But for some this book might be the starting place for your healing. Because I'm not a licensed counselor and this book doesn't take the place of therapy, please know there are some difficult realities in life that you will want a licensed Christian counselor to help you navigate. Please be honest about your need for counseling help. I am so thankful for the professionals who have lovingly helped lead me through my darkest days. It's always been important to me that the professional counselors I've seen have a deeply committed personal relationship with Jesus and who understand the battle must be fought in both the physical and spiritual realm. I'm praying for you, dear friend.

Much love,
Lysa

ACKNOWLEDGMENTS

When I was writing *It's Not Supposed to Be This Way*, there was a season I didn't think I had it in me to keep pressing through this project. I spent many hard days simply sitting on my bed contemplating moving to Montana to become a waitress. But I have amazing friends and family who see a different assignment for me. While being a waitress would be great, it's not my calling. And neither is being a CSI investigator, which has been my other secret option.

These friends have kept me focused on my assignments from God. They have held my hands, lifted my arms, and helped me carry this book to the finish line. To some really amazing people . . . I love you. And with everything in me, I thank you.

Art . . . the journey has been long and painful. But it's also been unexpectedly miraculous. Thank you for reading every word of this book and cheering me on to the finish line. I love you.

Jackson, Amanda, Mark, Selena, Susan Hope, Michael, Ashley, David, Brooke, Paige, and Philecia . . . my priority blessings and added blessings whom I love so very much.

Hamp, Colette, Wes, Laci, Pastor Rob and Michelle . . . I can only hope we can be there for others the way you've been there for us. I can't even think of the right word to describe the depth of your love. I'm simply speechless over the incredible way you live the gospel message.

Kristen, Shae, Hope, Kimberly and Amanda . . . I couldn't do this without your friendship, brilliant skills, and beautiful teamwork.

Meredith and Leah . . . the way you carry every one of my messages as if it was your own is a priceless gift to me.

Wendy B, Sharon S, Courtney D, Karen E, Krista W . . . thank you for praying me through the hardest season of my life.

Joel M . . . I don't ever want to write another book without you on my team. My favorite days are when Leah and I get to do theological studying with you. Thank you for your humble brilliance.

Kaley and Madi . . . you make everything beautiful that you touch. Thank you for helping design the set for this book's videos.

Alison, Meredith, Riley, Tori, Anna . . . you really are the most talented design team. Thank you for capturing the gentle balance between the felt need and the hope for healing in this book cover. You dressed my message beautifully and I am so grateful.

The Proverbs 31 Ministries team . . . the most dedicated and stellar people in ministry. It's an honor to work with you.

The P31 Board . . . incredible minds, dear friends.

Pastor and my family at Elevation . . . how do you do what you do every week? Thank you for your faithfulness.

Pastor Chris and Tammy . . . I treasure you both so very much. Thank you for welcoming me into your family with such unconditional love and acceptance.

Lisa C, Jeremy, and Lori G. . . . you are each answers to my prayers. I love doing life with you.

Michael Cusick with Restoring the Soul Counseling and Jim Cress, counselor . . . you are salt and light in the exact way my family needed it the most. You were there to help us survive the storm and walk forward with healing. Thank you.

Brian Hampton, Jessica Wong, Mark Schoenwald, Mark Glesne, Jessalyn Foggy, Janene MacIvor, Lori Lynch, Sara Broun, John Raymond, Sara Riemersma . . . you are truly publishing partners. You encourage me, challenge me, and help breathe life into every book I write. You aren't just ministry partners to me . . . you are lifelong friends.

The *It's Not Supposed to Be This Way* Early Reader Group . . . thank you so much for walking alongside me while I wrote every chapter. Your feedback and your love helped shape this message in the best of ways.

SCRIPTURES

INTRODUCTION

But thanks be to God! He gives us the victory through our Lord Jesus
Christ. (1 Corinthians 15:57)

CHAPTER 1: BETWEEN TWO GARDENS

"Look! God's dwelling place is now among the people, and he will dwell
with them. They will be his people, and God himself will be with them and
be their God. 'He will wipe every tear from their eyes. There will be no more
death' or mourning or crying or pain, for the old order of things has passed
away." He who was seated on the throne said, "I am making everything
new!" (Revelation 21:3–5)

CHAPTER 2: DUST

Then the Lord God formed a man from the dust of the ground and breathed
into his nostrils the breath of life, and the man became a living being.
(Genesis 2:7)

"While I am in the world, I am the light of the world." After saying this,
[Jesus] spit on the ground, made some mud with the saliva, and put it on
the man's eyes. (John 9:5–6)

Yet You, Lord, are our Father.

We are the clay, you are the potter;

we are all the work of your hand.

(Isaiah 64:8)

"Can I not do with you, Israel, as this potter does?" declares the Lord. "Like clay in the hand of the potter, so are you in my hand, Israel." (Jeremiah 18:6)

For we know that when this earthly tent we live in is taken down (that is, when we die and leave this earthly body), we will have a house in heaven, an eternal body made for us by God himself and not by human hands. We grow weary in our present bodies, and we long to put on our heavenly bodies like new clothing. For we will put on heavenly bodies; we will not be spirits without bodies. While we live in these earthly bodies, we groan and sigh, but it's not that we want to die and get rid of these bodies that clothe us. Rather, we want to put on our new bodies so that these dying bodies will be swallowed up by life. God himself has prepared us for this, and as a guarantee he has given us his Holy Spirit. (2 Corinthians 5:1–5 NLT)

[God's declaration about Eden restored:] "I am making everything new!" (Revelation 21:5)

CHAPTER 3: BUT HOW DO I GET THROUGH THE NEXT 86,400 SECONDS?

During the days of Jesus' life on earth, he offered up prayers and petitions with fervent cries and tears to the one who could save him from death, and he was heard because of his reverent submission. Son though he was, he learned obedience from what he suffered and, once made perfect, he became the source of eternal salvation for all who obey him. (Hebrews 5:7–9)

"Take this cup from me. Yet not what I will, but what you will." (Mark 14:36)

> "Our Father in heaven,
> hallowed be your name,
> your kingdom come,
> your will be done,
> on earth as it is in heaven.
> Give us today our daily bread."
> (Matthew 6:9–11)

Since the children have flesh and blood, he too shared in their humanity so that by his death he might break the power of him who holds the power of death—that is, the devil—and free those who all their lives were held in slavery by their fear of death . . . For this reason he had to be made like them, fully human in every way, in order that he might become a merciful and faithful high priest in service to God, and that he might make atonement for the sins of the people. Because he himself suffered when he was tempted, he is able to help those who are being tempted. (Hebrews 2:14–15, 17–18)

Therefore, holy brothers and sisters, who share in the heavenly calling, fix your thoughts on Jesus, whom we acknowledge as our apostle and high priest. (Hebrews 3:1)

> Hope deferred makes the heart sick,
> but a longing fulfilled is a tree of life.
> (Proverbs 13:12)

CHAPTER 4: TAN FEET

For the Spirit God gave us does not make us timid, but gives us power, love and self-disipline. (2 Timothy 1:7)

Adam and his wife were both naked, and they felt no shame. (Genesis 2:25)

But the Lord God called to the man, "Where are you?" . . .

And he said, "Who told you that you were naked? Have you eaten from the tree that I commanded you not to eat from?" (Genesis 3:9, 11)

CHAPTER 5: PAINTINGS AND PEOPLE

They triumphed over him by the blood of the Lamb and by the word of their testimony. (Revelation 12:11)

Praise be to the God and Father of our Lord Jesus Christ, the Father of compassion and the God of all comfort, who comforts us in all our troubles, so that we can comfort those in any trouble with the comfort we ourselves receive from God. (2 Corinthians 1:3–4)

Therefore, as God's chosen people, holy and dearly loved, clothe yourselves with compassion, kindness, humility, gentleness and patience. (Colossians 3:12)

CHAPTER 6: A LITTLE TOO LONG AND A LOT TOO HARD

I waited patiently for the LORD;
    he turned to me and heard my cry.
He lifted me out of the slimy pit,
    out of the mud and mire;
he set my feet on a rock
    and gave me a firm place to stand.
He put a new song in my mouth,
    a hymn of praise to our God.
Many will see and fear the LORD
    and put their trust in him.

Blessed is the one
who trusts in the LORD.
(Psalm 40:1–4)

After Job had prayed for his friends [the ones who misjudged Job, didn't tell the truth about God, and added so much hurt on top of Job's pain] the LORD restored his fortunes and gave him twice as much as he had before. (Job 42:10)

The LORD blessed the latter part of Job's life more than the former part. (Job 42:12)

Job lived a hundred and forty years; he saw his children and their children to the fourth generation. (Job 42:16)

And the God of all grace, who called you to his eternal glory in Christ, after you have suffered a little while, will himself restore you and make you strong, firm and steadfast. (1 Peter 5:10)

For this reason, since the day we heard about you, we have not stopped praying for you. We continually ask God to fill you with the knowledge of his will through all the wisdom and understanding that the Spirit gives, so that you may live a life worthy of the Lord and please him in every way: bearing fruit in every good work, growing in the knowledge of God, being strengthened with all power according to his glorious might so that you may have great endurance and patience. (Colossians 1:9–11)

But he said to me, "My grace is sufficient for you, for my power is made perfect in weakness." Therefore I will boast all the more gladly about my weaknesses, so that Christ's power may rest on me. That is why, for Christ's sake, I delight in weaknesses, in insults, in hardships, in persecutions, in difficulties. For when I am weak, then I am strong. (2 Corinthians 12:9–10)

Consider it pure joy, my brothers and sisters, whenever you face trials of many kinds, because you know that the testing of your faith produces perseverance. Let perseverance finish its work so that you may be mature and complete, not lacking anything. (James 1:2–4)

CHAPTER 7: WHEN GOD GIVES YOU MORE THAN YOU CAN HANDLE

No temptation has overtaken you except what is common to mankind. And God is faithful; he will not let you be tempted beyond what you can bear. But when you are tempted, he will also provide a way out so that you can endure it. (1 Corinthians 10:13)

For we do not want you to be uninformed, brothers and sisters, about the troubles we experienced in the province of Asia. We were under great pressure, far beyond our ability to endure, so that we despaired of life itself. Indeed, we felt we had received the sentence of death. But this happened that we might not rely on ourselves but on God, who raises the dead. (2 Corinthians 1:8–9)

Woe to those who quarrel with their Maker, those who are nothing but potsherds among the potsherds on the ground. Does the clay say to the potter, "What are you making?" Does your work say, "The potter has no hands"? (Isaiah 45:9)

So Satan went out from the presence of the LORD and afflicted Job with painful sores from the soles of his feet to the crown of his head. Then Job took a piece of broken pottery and scraped himself with it as he sat among the ashes.

His wife said to him, "Are you still maintaining your integrity? Curse God and die!"

He replied, "You are talking like a foolish woman. Shall we accept good from God, and not trouble?"

In all this, Job did not sin in what he said. (Job 2:7–10)

When seventy years are completed for Babylon, I will come to you and fulfill my good promise to bring you back to this place. For I know the plans I have for you . . . plans to prosper you and not to harm you, plans to give you hope and a future. Then you will call on me and come and pray to me, and I will listen to you. You will seek me and find me when you seek me with all your heart. I will be found by you. (Jeremiah 29:10–14)

Blessed are the pure in heart, for they will see God. (Matthew 5:8)

Listen to me . . . you whom I have upheld since your birth, and have carried since you were born. Even to your old age and gray hairs I am he, I am he who will sustain you. I have made you and I will carry you. I will sustain you and I will rescue you . . . I am God, and there is no other; I am God, and there is none like me. I make known the end from the beginning, from ancient times, what is still to come. I say, "My purpose will stand, and I will do all that I please." From the east I summon a bird of prey; from a far-off land, a man to fulfill my purpose. What I have said, that I will bring about; what I have planned, that I will do. (Isaiah 46:3–4, 9–11)

"I am the way and the truth and the life. No one comes to the Father except through me." (John 14:6)

He is the Maker of heaven and earth, the sea, and everything in them—he remains faithful forever. (Psalm 146:6)

So do not fear, for I am with you; do not be dismayed, for I am your God. I will strengthen you and help you; I will uphold you with my righteous right hand. (Isaiah 41:10)

> Yet I am always with you;
>> you hold me by my right hand.
>
> (Psalm 73:23)

> You are my hiding place;
>> you will protect me from trouble
>> and surround me with songs of deliverance.
>
> (Psalm 32:7)

CHAPTER 8: LETTING GO OF WHAT'S HOLDING ME BACK

> Guide me in your truth and teach me,
>> for you are God my Savior,
>> and my hope is in you all day long.
>
> (Psalm 25:5)

Therefore, since we are surrounded by such a great cloud of witnesses, let us throw off everything that hinders and the sin that so easily entangles. And let us run with perseverance the race marked out for us, fixing our eyes on Jesus, the pioneer and perfecter of faith. For the joy set before him he endured the cross, scorning its shame, and sat down at the right hand of the throne of God. (Hebrews 12:1–2)

As he went along, he saw a man blind from birth. His disciples asked him, "Rabbi, who sinned, this man or his parents, that he was born blind?"

"Neither this man nor his parents sinned," said Jesus, "but this happened so that the works of God might be displayed in him. As long as it is day, we must do the works of him who sent me. Night is coming, when no one can work. While I am in the world, I am the light of the world."

After saying this, he spit on the ground, made some mud with the saliva, and put it on the man's eyes. "Go," he told him, "wash in the Pool of Siloam" (this word means "Sent"). So the man went and washed, and came home seeing. (John 9:1–7)

Jesus heard that they had thrown him out, and when he found him, he said, "Do you believe in the Son of Man?"

"Who is he, sir?" the man asked. "Tell me so that I may believe in him."

Jesus said, "You have now seen him; in fact, he is the one speaking with you."

Then the man said, "Lord, I believe," and he worshiped him. (John 9:35–38)

> Have mercy on me, O God,
>> according to your unfailing love;
> according to your great compassion
>> blot out my transgressions.
> Wash away all my iniquity
>> and cleanse me from my sin.
>
> For I know my transgressions
>> and my sin is always before me.
> Against you, you only, have I sinned
>> and done what is evil in your sight;
> so you are right in your verdict
>> and justified when you judge.
> Surely I was sinful at birth,
>> sinful from the time my mother conceived me.

Yet you desired faithfulness even in the womb;
  you taught me wisdom in that secret place.

Cleanse me with hyssop, and I will be clean;
  wash me, and I will be whiter than snow.
Let me hear joy and gladness;
  let the bones you have crushed rejoice.
Hide your face from my sins
  and blot out all my iniquity.

Create in me a pure heart, O God,
  and renew a steadfast spirit within me.
Do not cast me from your presence
  or take your Holy Spirit from me.
Restore to me the joy of your salvation
  and grant me a willing spirit, to sustain me.

Then I will teach transgressors your ways,
  so that sinners will turn back to you.
Deliver me from the guilt of bloodshed, O God,
  you who are God my Savior,
  and my tongue will sing of your righteousness.
Open my lips, Lord,
  and my mouth will declare your praise.
(Psalm 51:1–15)

Do you see what this means—all these pioneers who blazed the way, all these veterans cheering us on? It means we'd better get on with it. Strip down, start running—and never quit! No extra spiritual fat, no parasitic sins. Keep your eyes on Jesus, who both began and finished this race we're in. Study how he did it. Because he never lost sight of where he was headed—that exhilarating finish in and with God—he could put up with anything along the way: Cross, shame, whatever. And now he's there, in the place of honor, right alongside God. When you find yourselves flagging in your faith, go over that story again, item by item, that long litany of hostility he plowed through. That will shoot adrenaline into your souls! (Hebrews 12:1–3 The Message)

Therefore, since we have been justified through faith, we have peace with God through our Lord Jesus Christ, through whom we have gained access by faith into this grace in which we now stand. And we boast in the hope of the glory of God. Not only so, but we also glory in our sufferings, because we know that suffering produces perseverance; perseverance, character; and character, hope. (Romans 5:1–4)

CHAPTER 9: EXPOSING THE ENEMY

The thief comes only to steal and kill and destroy; I have come that they may have life, and have it to the full. (John 10:10)

When tempted, no one should say, "God is tempting me." For God cannot be tempted by evil, nor does he tempt anyone; but each person is tempted when they are dragged away by their own evil desire and enticed. Then, after desire has conceived, it gives birth to sin; and sin, when it is full-grown, gives birth to death.

Don't be deceived, my dear brothers and sisters . . .

Therefore, get rid of all moral filth and the evil that is so prevalent and humbly accept the word planted in you, which can save you.

Do not merely listen to the word, and so deceive yourselves. Do what it says. (James 1:13–16, 21–22)

For the word of God is alive and active. Sharper than any double-edged sword, it penetrates even to dividing soul and spirit, joints and marrow; it judges the thoughts and attitudes of the heart. Nothing in all creation is hidden from God's sight. Everything is uncovered and laid bare before the eyes of him to whom we must give account.

Therefore, since we have a great high priest who has ascended into heaven, Jesus the Son of God, let us hold firmly to the faith we profess. For we do not have a high priest who is unable to empathize with our weaknesses, but we have one who has been tempted in every way, just as we are—yet he did not sin. Let us then approach God's throne of grace with confidence, so that we may receive mercy and find grace to help us in our time of need. (Hebrews 4:12–16)

These people are springs without water and mists driven by a storm. Blackest darkness is reserved for them. For they mouth empty, boastful words and, by appealing to the lustful desires of the flesh, they entice people who are just escaping from those who live in error. They promise them freedom while they themselves are slaves of depravity—for "people are slaves to whatever has mastered them." (2 Peter 2:17–19)

The Lord is not slow in keeping his promise, as some understand slowness. Instead he is patient with you, not wanting anyone to perish, but everyone to come to repentance. (2 Peter 3:9)

Do not be deceived: God cannot be mocked. A man reaps what he sows. Whoever sows to please their flesh, from the flesh will reap destruction; whoever sows to please the Spirit, from the Spirit will reap eternal life. (Galatians 6:7–8)

"I have the right to do anything," you say—but not everything is beneficial.

"I have the right to do anything"—but not everything is constructive. (1 Corinthians 10:23)

As for you, you were dead in your transgressions and sins, in which you used to live when you followed the ways of this world and of the ruler of the kingdom of the air, the spirit who is now at work in those who are disobedient. All of us also lived among them at one time, gratifying the cravings of our flesh and following its desires and thoughts. Like the rest, we were by nature deserving of wrath. But because of his great love for us, God, who is rich in mercy, made us alive with Christ even when we were dead in transgressions—it is by grace you have been saved. (Ephesians 2:1–5)

Through these he has given us his very great and precious promises, so that through them you may participate in the divine nature, having escaped the corruption in the world caused by evil desires. (2 Peter 1:4)

Don't be deceived, my dear brothers and sisters. Every good and perfect gift is from above, coming down from the Father of the heavenly lights, who does not change like shifting shadows. (James 1:16–17)

> The heart is deceitful above all things
>   and beyond cure.
>   Who can understand it?
> (Jeremiah 17:9)

> May these words of my mouth and this meditation of my heart
>   be pleasing in your sight,
>   LORD, my Rock and my Redeemer.
> (Psalm 19:14)

> Now have come the salvation and the power
>   and the kingdom of our God,

and the authority of his Messiah.

For the accuser of our brothers and sisters,

who accuses them before our God day and night,

has been hurled down.

They triumphed over him

by the blood of the Lamb

and by the word of their testimony;

they did not love their lives so much

as to shrink from death.

(Revelation 12:10–11)

So the Lord God said to the serpent:

"Because you have done this,

You are cursed more than all cattle,

And more than every beast of the field;

On your belly you shall go,

And you shall eat dust

All the days of your life."

(Genesis 3:14 NKJV)

In all this you greatly rejoice, though now for a little while you may have had to suffer grief in all kinds of trials. **These have come so that the proven genuineness of your faith**—of greater worth than gold, which perishes even though refined by fire—**may result in praise, glory and honor when Jesus Christ is revealed.** (1 Peter 1:6–7, emphasis mine)

Therefore, with minds that are alert and fully sober, set your hope on the grace to be brought to you when Jesus Christ is revealed at his coming. As obedient children, do not conform to the evil desires you had when you lived in ignorance. But just as he who called you is holy, so be holy in all you do; for it is written: "Be holy, because I am holy." (1 Peter 1:13–16)

Is anyone among you in trouble? Let them pray. Is anyone happy? Let them sing songs of praise. Is anyone among you sick? Let them call the elders of the church to pray over them and anoint them with oil in the name of the Lord. And the prayer offered in faith will make the sick person well; the Lord will raise them up. If they have sinned, they will be forgiven. Therefore confess your sins to each other and pray for each other so that you may be healed. The prayer of a righteous person is powerful and effective. (James 5:13–16)

Who is going to harm you if you are eager to do good? But even if you should suffer for what is right, you are blessed. "Do not fear their threats; do not be frightened." But in your hearts revere Christ as Lord. Always be prepared to give an answer to everyone who asks you to give the reason for the hope that you have. But do this with gentleness and respect, keeping a clear conscience, so that those who speak maliciously against your good behavior in Christ may be ashamed of their slander. For it is better, if it is God's will, to suffer for doing good than for doing evil. (1 Peter 3:13–17)

CHAPTER 10: FIGHTING WORDS

"I have told you these things, so that in me you may have peace. In this world you will have trouble. But take heart! I have overcome the world." (John 16:33)

But seek first his kingdom and his righteousness, and all these things will be given to you as well. Therefore do not worry about tomorrow, for tomorrow will worry about itself. Each day has enough trouble of its own." (Matthew 6:33–34)

Dear friends, do not be surprised at the fiery ordeal that has come on you to test you, as though something strange were happening to you. But rejoice inasmuch as you participate in the sufferings of Christ, so that you may be overjoyed when his glory is revealed. (1 Peter 4:12–13)

Moab has been at rest from youth, like wine left on its dregs, not poured from one jar to another—she has not gone into exile. So she tastes as she did, and her aroma is unchanged. (Jeremiah 48:11)

Those who live according to the flesh have their minds set on what the flesh desires; but those who live in accordance with the Spirit have their minds set on what the Spirit desires. The mind governed by the flesh is death, but the mind governed by the Spirit is life and peace. (Romans 8:5–6)

Do not conform to the pattern of this world, but be transformed by the renewing of your mind. Then you will be able to test and approve what God's will is—his good, pleasing and perfect will. (Romans 12:2)

We have heard of the glories of Moab, of its excessive pride and its boasting, of its outbursts of false propaganda. For this shall the Moabites be made to lament, and all have cause to bewail Moab: they shall groan at the ruin of Kir Hareseth in utter dejection. . . . The joyful festivity will be gone from the orchards; no shouts of delight shall sound in the vineyards. The wine treaders will tread no wine in the presses; the vintage shout I will bring to an end. (Isaiah 16:6–7, 10 IIT)

> But now, this is what the LORD, your Creator says, O Jacob,
> And He who formed you, O Israel,
> "Do not fear, for I have redeemed you [from captivity];
> I have called you by name; you are Mine!

"When you pass through the waters, I will be with you;
And through the rivers, they will not overwhelm you.
When you walk through fire, you will not be scorched,
Nor will the flame burn you.

"For I am the Lord your God,
The Holy One of Israel, your Savior;
I have given Egypt [to the Babylonians] as your ransom,
Cush (ancient Ethiopia) and Seba [its province] in exchange
     for you.

"Because you are precious in My sight,
You are honored and I love you,
I will give *other* men in return for you and *other* peoples in
     exchange for your life.

"Do not fear, for I am with you."
(Isaiah 43:1–5 AMP)

Forget the former things;
     do not dwell on the past.
See, I am doing a new thing!
     Now it springs up; do you not perceive it?
I am making a way in the wilderness
     and streams in the wasteland.
(Isaiah 43:18–19)

God will strengthen you with his own great power so that you will not give up when troubles come, but you will be patient. (Colossians 1:11 NCV)

The Lord is near to all who call on him,
to all who call on him in truth.

(Psalm 145:18)

Yet this I call to mind
and therefore I have hope:

Because of the LORD's great love we are not consumed,
for his compassions never fail.
They are new every morning;
great is your faithfulness.

(Lamentations 3:21–23)

"I have much more to say to you, more than you can now bear. But when he, the Spirit of truth, comes, he will guide you into all the truth. He will not speak on his own; he will speak only what he hears, and he will tell you what is yet to come. He will glorify me because it is from me that he will receive what he will make known to you. All that belongs to the Father is mine. That is why I said the Spirit will receive from me what he will make known to you." (John 16:12–15)

"Because he loves me," says the LORD, "I will rescue him;
I will protect him, for he acknowledges my name.
He will call on me, and I will answer him;
I will be with him in trouble,
I will deliver him and honor him."

(Psalm 91:14–15)

"I will give them a heart to know me, that I am the LORD. They will be my people, and I will be their God, for they will return to me with all their heart." (Jeremiah 24:7)

They will have no fear of bad news;

their hearts are steadfast, trusting in the LORD.

(Psalm 112:7)

May these words of my mouth and this meditation of my heart

be pleasing in your sight,

LORD, my Rock and my Redeemer.

(Psalm 19:14)

Is anyone among you suffering? *Then* he must pray. Is anyone cheerful? He is to sing praises. (James 5:13 NASB)

I will praise you, LORD, with all my heart;

before the "gods" I will sing your praise.

I will bow down toward your holy temple

and will praise your name

for your unfailing love and your faithfulness,

for you have so exalted your solemn decree

that it surpasses your fame.

When I called, you answered me;

you greatly emboldened me. . . .

Though I walk in the midst of trouble,

you preserve my life.

You stretch out your hand against the anger of my foes;

with your right hand you save me.

(Psalm 138:1–3, 7)

You will keep in perfect peace

those whose minds are steadfast,

because they trust in you.

(Isaiah 26:3)

Be alert and of sober mind. Your enemy the devil prowls around like a roaring lion looking for someone to devour. (1 Peter 5:8)

> My son, pay attention to my wisdom,
>   turn your ear to my words of insight,
> that you may maintain discretion
>   and your lips may preserve knowledge.
> (Proverbs 5:1–2)

> Let your eyes look directly ahead [toward the path of moral
>   courage]
> And let your gaze be fixed straight in front of you [toward the
>   path of integrity].

> Consider well *and* watch carefully the path of your feet,
> And all your ways will be steadfast *and* sure.

> Do not turn away to the right nor to the left [where evil may
>   lurk];
> Turn your foot from [the path of] evil.
> (Proverbs 4:25–27 AMP)

So let's keep focused on that goal, those of us who want everything God has for us. If any of you have something else in mind, something less than total commitment, God will clear your blurred vision—you'll see it yet! Now that we're on the right track, let's stay on it.

Stick with me, friends. Keep track of those you see running this same course, headed for this same goal. There are many out there taking other paths, choosing other goals, and trying to get you to go along with them. I've warned you of them many times; sadly, I'm having to do it again. All they want is easy street. They hate Christ's Cross. But easy street is a dead-end street. Those who live there make their bellies their gods; belches are their praise; all they can think of is their appetites.

But there's far more to life for us. We're citizens of high heaven! We're waiting the arrival of the Savior, the Master, Jesus Christ, who will transform our earthy bodies into glorious bodies like his own. He'll make us beautiful and whole with the same powerful skill by which he is putting everything as it should be, under and around him. (Philippians 3:15–21 THE MESSAGE)

For everything in the world—the lust of the flesh, the lust of the eyes, and the pride of life—comes not from the Father but from the world. (1 John 2:16)

Therefore, holy brothers and sisters, who share in the heavenly calling, fix your thoughts on Jesus, whom we acknowledge as our apostle and high priest. (Hebrews 3:1)

Do you see what this means—all these pioneers who blazed the way, all these veterans cheering us on? It means we'd better get on with it. Strip down, start running—and never quit! No extra spiritual fat, no parasitic sins. Keep your eyes on *Jesus*, who both began and finished this race we're in. Study how he did it. Because he never lost sight of where he was headed—that exhilarating finish in and with God—he could put up with anything along the way: Cross, shame, whatever. And now he's *there*, in the place of honor, right alongside God. (Hebrews 12:1–2 THE MESSAGE)

For we are God's handiwork, created in Christ Jesus to do good works, which God prepared in advance for us to do. (Ephesians 2:10)

So then, brothers and sisters, stand firm and hold fast to the teachings we passed on to you, whether by word of mouth or by letter. May our Lord Jesus Christ himself and God our Father, who loved us and by his grace gave us eternal encouragement and good hope, encourage your hearts and strengthen you in every good deed and word. (2 Thessalonians 2:15–17)

Therefore, my fellow believers, whom I love and long for, my delight and crown [my wreath of victory], in this way stand firm in the Lord, my beloved . . . Do not be anxious *or* worried about anything, but in everything [every circumstance and situation] by prayer and petition with thanksgiving, continue to make your [specific] requests known to God. And the peace of God [that peace which reassures the heart, that peace] which transcends all understanding, [that peace which] stands guard over your hearts and your minds in Christ Jesus [is yours]. Finally, believers, whatever is true, whatever is honorable *and* worthy of respect, whatever is right *and* confirmed by God's word, whatever is pure *and* wholesome, whatever is lovely *and* brings peace, whatever is admirable *and* of good repute; if there is any excellence, if there is anything worthy of praise, think *continually* on these things [center your mind on them, and implant them in your heart]. (Philippians 4:1, 6–8 AMP)

God is not human, that he should lie, not a human being, that he should change his mind. Does he speak and then not act? Does he promise and not fulfill? (Numbers 23:19)

CHAPTER 11: UPSIDE DOWN

Consider it pure joy, my brothers and sisters, whenever you face trials of many kinds, because you know that the testing of your faith produces perseverance. Let perseverance finish its work so that you may be mature and complete, not lacking anything. (James 1:2–4)

Blessed is the one who perseveres under trial because, having stood the test, that person will receive the crown of life that the Lord has promised to those who love him. (James 1:12)

AN INVITATION

You're invited . . . Lysa's doing some small, upcoming gatherings to show you how to go more in-depth with these teachings and make them personally applicable to your life. If you'd like to be added to the interest list, please visit https://lysaterkeurst.com/invitation-from-lysa.

NOTES

1. C. S. Lewis, "Is Theology Poetry?" in *The Weight of Glory: And Other Addresses* (New York: HarperCollins, 2001), 140.
2. C. H. Spurgeon, "Christ the Tree of Life," in *The Metropolitan Tabernacle Pulpit Sermons*, vol. 57 (London: Passmore & Alabaster, 1911), 242, 245.
3. David Bayles and Ted Orland, *Art & Fear* (Image Continuum, 1993), 4.
4. Conversation with Jessica Leavitt.
5. Ravi Zaccharias, Good Reads, accessed June 3, 2018, https://www .goodreads.com/quotes/746709-sin-will-take-you-farther-than-you -want-to-go.
6. Carl Wieland, "Snakes Do Eat Dust," *Creation* 10, no. 4 (September 1988), 38, https://creation.com/snakes-do-eat-dust.

ABOUT THE AUTHOR

Amy Riley Wobser

LYSA TERKEURST is the president of Proverbs 31 Ministries and the #1 *New York Times* bestselling author of *Uninvited, The Best Yes,* and twenty other books. But to those who know her best she's just a simple girl with a well-worn Bible who proclaims hope in the midst of good times and heart-breaking realities.

Lysa lives with her family in Charlotte, North Carolina. Connect with her on a daily basis, see pictures of her family, and follow her speaking schedule:

Blog: www.LysaTerKeurst.com
(Click on "speaking" to inquire about having Lysa speak at your event.)
Facebook: www.Facebook.com/OfficialLysa
Instagram: @LysaTerKeurst
Twitter: @LysaTerKeurst

If you enjoyed *It's Not Supposed to Be This Way*, equip yourself with additional resources at www.ItsNotSupposedToBeThisWay.com, www.LysaTerKeurst.com, and www.Proverbs31.org.

FREE GIFTS FOR YOU!

Are you looking for Truth to cling to when life seems impossibly hard and God feels far away?

"Bonus Fighting Words"

Be equipped with even more declarations to speak over the parts of your life that are most vulnerable to attacks from the enemy with these BONUS Fighting Words!

Download your printable, designed version at https://proverbs31.org/gifts-for-you.

"A Prayer of Restoration"

Continue to pray for healing over your deepest disappointments with Lysa's "Prayer of Restoration" that she has personally spoken over her own hard realities in need of being restored.

Visit https://proverbs31.org/gifts-for-you to download your copy today.

About Proverbs 31 Ministries

Lysa TerKeurst is the president of Proverbs 31 Ministries, located in Charlotte, North Carolina.

If you were inspired by *It's Not Supposed to Be This Way* and desire to deepen your own personal relationship with Jesus Christ, we have just what you're looking for.

Proverbs 31 Ministries exists to be a trusted friend who will take you by the hand and walk by your side, leading you one step closer to the heart of God through:

Free *First 5* app

Free online daily devotions

Online Bible studies

Writer and speaker training

Daily radio programs

Books and resources

For more information about Proverbs 31 Ministries, visit www.Proverbs31.org.

To inquire about having Lysa speak at your event, visit www.LysaTerKeurst.com and click on "speaking."

Don't miss the video series and study guide for *It's Not Supposed to Be This Way*

Filmed at Lysa's home, this six-session video series is perfect for your Bible study, book club, small group, or individual use. Join Lysa TerKeurst as she unpacks the Scriptures even more fully and helps apply the teaching to your specific situations. The study guide includes video notes, group discussion questions, and activities for groups, plus personal study and reflection materials for in-between sessions.

Study Guide
9780310094340

DVD
9780310094364

Available now at your favorite bookstore, or streaming video on StudyGateway.com.

"Rejection steals the best of who I am by reinforcing the worst of what's been said to me."

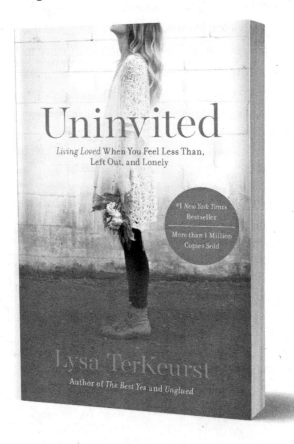

With biblical depth, gut-honest vulnerability, and refreshing wit, Lysa will help you stop feeling left out by believing that even when you are overlooked by others you are handpicked by God.

www.Uninvitedbook.com